Implementation of Environmental Policies in Developing Countries

Implementation of Environmental Policies in Developing Countries

A Case of Protected Areas and Tourism in Brazil

Jose Antonio Puppim de Oliveira

STATE UNIVERSITY OF NEW YORK PRESS

Cover photo credit, istockphoto/March Rigaud

Published by
State University of New York Press, Albany

© 2008 State University of New York

For information, contact State University of New York Press, Albany, NY
www.sunypress.edu

Production by Kelli W. LeRoux
Marketing by Michael Campochiaro

Library of Congress Cataloging-in-Publication Data

Puppim de Oliveira, Jose Antonio.
    Implementation of environmental policies in developing countries : a
case of protected areas and tourism in Brazil / Jose Antonio Puppim de Oliveira.
        p. cm. — (SUNY series in global environmental policy)
    Includes bibliographical references and index.
    ISBN 978-0-7914-7325-2 (hardcover : alk. paper)
    1. Environmental policy—Brazil.   2. Environmental management—Brazil.
3. Environmental protection—Brazil.   4. Tourism—Environmental aspects—Brazil.
5. Environmental policy—Developing countries.   6. Developing countries—
Environmental conditions.   I. Title.

GE190.B6O55 2008
333.720981—dc22   2007024543

                        10 9 8 7 6 5 4 3 2 1

Contents

List of Tables

List of Figures

List of Abbreviations

APA, Environmentally Protected Area, or Área de Proteção Ambiental

BAHIATURSA, Bahia Tourism Authority, or Bahia Turismo S.A.

CEPRAM, State Environmental Council, or Conselho Estadual de Meio Ambiente

CONAMA, National Environmental Council, or Conselho Nacional do Meio Ambiente

CONDER, Company for the Development of the Metropolitan Region, or Companhia de Desenvolvimento da Região Metropolitana

CRA, Bahia State Environmental Agency, or Centro de Recursos Ambientais

IBAMA, Federal Environmental Agency, or Instituto Brasileiro do Meio Ambiente e dos Recursos Naturais Renováveis

IDB, Inter-American Development Bank

MMA, Ministry of the Environment, or Ministério do Meio Ambiente, Recursos Hídricos e da Amazônia Legal

NGO, Nongovernmental organization

ODA, Overseas Development Agency

PRODETUR, Tourism Development Program, or Programa de Desenvolvimento do Turismo

SECTUR, State Secretariat of Culture and Tourism, or Secretaria de Cultura e Turismo

SEPLANTEC, State Secretariat of Planing, Science, and Technology, or Secretaria de Planejamento, Ciência e Tecnologia

Acknowledgments

This book is the result of years of research work and reflections about environmental policy implementation in developing countries, which also produced a doctoral thesis and several journal articles.[1] Although the writing and ideas (including the errors) were my sole responsibility, the task would not have been possible without the academic and personal advice and support of several people and organizations. I am grateful to the Department of Urban Studies and Planning at the Massachusetts Institute of Technology (MIT) for the invaluable academic guidance and financial support through the Voorhees Scholarship. I pay homage to the late Rolf Engler for ensuring this funding was used wisely. I would like to especially thank Larry Susskind, for his continuing support since the beginning of my academic and professional life. His comments on the first versions of the manuscript and precious advice, both on how to do and write research, were crucial to this book. I also express my gratitude to Judith Tendler for institutional support and comments on the early versions; from her I gained insights about in-depth empirical research and learned to be critical in writing and analyzing the research findings.

I am beholden to the Brazilian Bank of the Northeast (BN, Banco do Nordeste) for the one-year research grant that allowed me to do most of my field research in Bahia and the Brazilian Northeast. I am particularly grateful to Myrtis Arrais de Souza, Everton Chaves Correia, and Adriano Sarquis Bezerra de Menezes for giving me the opportunity to work in such a friendly environment as BN. I also express my thanks to the staff of the State Environmental Agency (CRA) of Bahia for their openness and institutional support during my field research along the years. I am particularly grateful to Durval Olivieri, former director of CRA, for his support and vital information on the stories of environmentally protected areas (APAs).

I thank the Brazilian School of Public and Business Administration (EBAPE) of the Getulio Vargas Foundation (FGV) for providing a good institutional environment to write a book over several years. I especially single out Bianor Scelza Cavalcanti, Deborah Zouain, and Armando Cunha for their support at the beginning of my new academic life.

The encouragement of my wife Ana Rosa, my son Fernando and my daughter Bárbara was fundamental to not give up in the middle of the book. My parents, Any and Jose, and my extended family (Isabela, Poliana, Yasmin, Mateus, Maria Luisa, Monica, Regina, Vinicius, Magna, Marco, and Sergio) gave me the support I needed. I am indebted to them for the time I spent writing the book instead of being with them.

1

Introduction

This book is about implementation of environmental policy in developing countries. The book uses the case of protected areas to understand the main institutional obstacles to effective policy implementation and possible ways to overcome them. One key question concerns the role of government in trying to foster economic development and environmental protection at the same time.

Environmental problems in developing countries stem from both economic development and the lack of it. The modern, affluent segment of developing countries consumes large amounts of energy and natural resources and produces waste at a rate similar to that of developed countries. As countries achieve rapid economic growth, these problems tend to intensify. In contrast, widespread poverty causes other kinds of environmental problems, such as water pollution from the lack of sanitation in urban areas and deforestation from unsustainable slash-and-burn agriculture of poor peasants.

Thus environmental protection and economic development are linked but not linearly. More economic development does not necessarily mean more environmental impacts of all kinds, and less economic development does not necessarily mean that there will be no environmental impact. In this context, government has a dual mandate. On the one hand, governments are in charge of designing policies to spur economic development. On the other hand, government is responsible for protecting the environment in most countries, and the way they foster economic development can help or hurt. Nowadays, any development action has an environmental impact, and vice versa, and these

1

roles often conflict. This book attempts to analyze the conditions under which these mandates can be compatible.

In developing countries, rapid economic development is often the highest government priority. Pressured by low incomes, governments create different kinds of policies to foster economic growth. As a result, development-oriented agencies tend to be politically influential and powerful. They usually receive large amounts of funding to perform their tasks compared with nondevelopment agencies. Environmental agencies and issues, in contrast, often obtain little funding because they are not a political priority or because they involve highly politicized actions, such as expropriating land or restricting development. The puzzle in this book is to understand under what conditions and under what institutional arrangement governments tend to prioritize environmental concerns in their development agenda.

Another question is which institutional arrangement governments can use to implement environmental policies effectively. In the past, policies pursued under highly centralized governments often resulted in failure. Decentralization showed promise as a way to increase government efficiency and accountability. However, most of the literature has tended to look at how to decentralizing government tasks to lower levels of government, instead of examining different ways of decentralizing and whether decentralized governments implement policies effectively. This book focuses on how environmental policies are implemented in a decentralized manner, through decentralization at the same governmental level and in some degree of devolution to lower governmental levels.

The book examines the main institutional obstacles to effective environmental policy implementation in developing countries, focusing on the creation of protected areas. Governments usually fail to implement environmental policies because key implementing agencies lack political support, financial resources, institutional capacity, and coordination at the local level. I am particularly interested in understanding how and why, in some cases, governments have been able to overcome obstacles to create environmentally protected areas.

This research attempts to make several key contributions to the field of environmental policy implementation. First, the book argues that placing environmental protection in the mainstream development agenda seems to be at the core of the solution to try to overcome the obstacles mentioned above. Second, it provides one practical alternative to mainstreaming environmental policies: transferring some of the responsibilities to implement environmental policies to development-oriented agencies. For example, growing interest in nature-based tourism has stimulated governments in developing countries to create and manage protected areas through development agencies, such as tourism, planning, and urban development agencies. Third, the study "rediscovers" a forgotten form of decentralization in the literature: the "horizontal decentralization" (decentralizing the same task to several agencies at the same government level). This means that several agencies, instead of a central one, may implement the same environmental policies simultaneously more effectively, under certain conditions. Fourth, the study detects the two main conditions that should be in place to make development-oriented agencies to implement environmental policies adequately: the provision of incentives to the implementing agencies to do the environmental job and the existence of an independent system of checks and balances. Fifth, the book provides a framework for analyzing environmental policy implementation based on four obstacles governments should overcome to implement policies effectively: the lack of political support, financial resources, institutional capacity, and/or coordination at the local level. Finally, the book highlights the need for more in-depth empirical studies of implementation of protected area policies. This case study of Bahia, Brazil, shows how the involvement of development agencies in the creation of protected areas was able to overcome several of the political, institutional, and financial obstacles to policy implementation.

1.1 THE CASE STUDY

As in many parts of the developing world, local and state governments in Northeastern Brazil[1]—the most economically disadvantaged area of the country—want to spur rapid economic development. Since the end of the 1980s, this region has adopted tourism as one of its top economic development strategies. Federal, state, and local governments have invested several million dollars in tourism infrastructure and expected this investment to be matched by considerable investment from the private sector. Bahia, the largest of the Northeast's nine states (Figure 1.1), invested heavily in tourism-related projects in the 1990s (Bahia State Government, 1997).

Tourists come to the Bahian coast searching for scenic beaches and dunes and tropical settings framed by coconut trees and picturesque villages. Together with the region's cultural richness, coastal destinations are some of the most important tourist attractions in Bahia. On the other hand, tourism has exerted a series of negative impacts on the natural environment. These are likely to hinder tourist activity itself and hurt the region's economy if they are not managed well. Therefore, to be successful, tourism-related activity in a region like the Bahian coast depends on preservation of the area's natural resources. Local and state governments in Bahia responded to internal and external pressures to increase environmental protection while encouraging tourism to expand. To fulfill this dual mandate, the state government of Bahia created a significant number of *environmentally protected areas* (APAs[2]) in the1990s—one type of protected area. Between 1992 and 1998, the number of APAs increased by 1,200 percent, and their area multiplied by 130 (CRA, 2004).

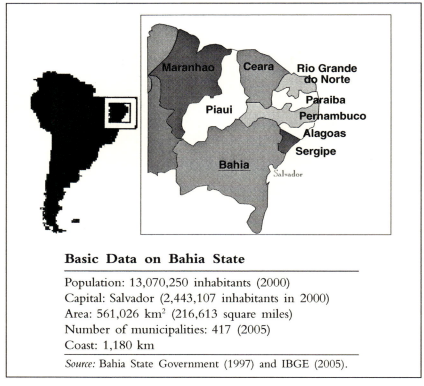

Basic Data on Bahia State

Population: 13,070,250 inhabitants (2000)
Capital: Salvador (2,443,107 inhabitants in 2000)
Area: 561,026 km² (216,613 square miles)
Number of municipalities: 417 (2005)
Coast: 1,180 km

Source: Bahia State Government (1997) and IBGE (2005).

Figure 1.1 The Brazilian Northeast and Bahia. *Source:* SUDENE, 1999.

APAs transfer certain development rights from private landowners and municipal governments to a group of actors composed of state and municipal governments as well as members of the local civil society, according to plans coordinated by state agencies. APAs permit the state government and civil society to interfere in matters usually handled by municipal governments, which are responsible for land-use planning. However, unlike areas under stricter conservation guidelines, such as state and national parks, no land expropriation is necessary to create an APA. This means that the financial burden of buying land is avoided, as well as possible conflicts with private landowners.

Especially in the 1990s, the creation of APAs became very common. One push for the creation of such areas was the environmental protection demands of federal and multilateral banks (such as the Bank of the Northeast[3] and the Inter-American Development Bank). For state agencies to obtain large loans from these banks for investment in infrastructure for tourism, the agencies had to comply with environmental requirements. Local governments, developers, and landowners eager to attract private tourism-related investment did not oppose the loss of some of their unfettered development rights, as they saw APAs as protecting their investments. Environmental groups also increasingly influenced public policymaking around the same time, because of the country's democratization process.

In this study, I examine the creation of APAs and the extent to which the government of Bahia was able to overcome the political, institutional, and financial obstacles to establishing and managing them. I explain what organizational arrangement led to the successful creation of APAs at the state level.

This study uses a combination of quantitative data and qualitative information drawn from semistructured interviews with government officials at the federal, state, and local level; local citizenry; members of nongovernmental organizations (NGOs); academics; and developers. As it turned out, I needed to make sense of the stories that took place in Bahia. I pieced together most of this story by talking to officials in the state capital, Salvador, and in the regions affected by the APAs. This story explains how different policy actors interacted to overcome the usual barriers to establishing protected areas. The case shows empirically under what conditions APAs were established.

1.2   ARGUMENTS IN BRIEF

Tourism has become an important economic activity in many parts of the world (WTO, 1999). Improvements in transportation and increasing incomes and vacation time have allowed more people to travel more often to more distant places (Tyler, 1989). Today, most parts of the world can be readily reached. One important feature of modern tourism is the growing popularity of nature-based tourism (Boo, 1990; Honey, 1999). This kind of tourism offers an appealing form of economic activity, especially for developing countries rich in environmental resources. However, the quick disappearance of the natural environment owing to unrestrained development—some of which is due to tourism itself— poses a threat to the sustainability of such activity in places that have just begun to enjoy its benefits.

Government-managed protected areas have therefore emerged as one of the main types of tourist destinations. Besides promoting them as tourist attractions, many governments have relied on protected areas to control land development and preserve rare fauna and flora. In some developing countries, however, public agencies have had difficulty establishing and managing significant numbers of protected areas. This is partly because they lack many of the financial, institutional, and political resources needed to create and maintain them and fend off powerful development interests. Still, some governments have been able to create and manage protected areas.

This study examines why and how some governments have supported protected-area policies and have been able to overcome the political, institutional, and financial obstacles to establishing and maintaining them. I am particularly interested in understanding how the rise of the environmental movement and growing international interest in nature-based tourism can stimulate the creation and effective management of protected areas in developing countries.

In this book, I develop an analytical framework for understanding the obstacles to implement environmental policies, using the case of the establishment of protected areas (see Chapter 3). Based on the literature of protected-area policy and management, I identify four main obstacles to the creation and management of protected areas: the lack of political support, financial resources, institutional capacity, and/or cooperation from local actors. In my case study of Bahia, I use this analytical framework to understand why and to what extent Bahia was capable of overcoming these obstacles to create and manage a considerable number of protected areas. This research adds to the scarce literature on protected areas in developing countries. That literature mostly provides normative recommendations or descriptive analyses (Ceballos-Lascurain, 1996; McNeely, 1993) of protected areas. The lack of empirical research has made it difficult to understand how protected areas are established and managed in the field, as well as integrated with development policies.

Decentralization of decision making turns out to be key in the story. Had Bahia state government not allocated responsibility for creating and administering APAs to a variety of state and local agencies, it would not have been possible to create such a large number of APAs. Horizontal decentralization allowed an increase in the state capacity for creating protected areas. Instead of centralizing power in the hands of a single state environmental agency (CRA), the government allowed other state agencies to initiate APAs on their own—especially the State Secretariat of Culture and Tourism (Sectur) and the Company for the Development of the Metropolitan Region (Companhia de Desenvolvimento da Regiao Metropolitana, or Conder).

Overall, the effects of decentralization were fourfold, tackling the four obstacles to establishing protected areas examined in the analytical framework in Chapter 3. First, political support for creating APAs grew as development agencies promoted APA policy instead of blocking it. Second, state-level decentralization attracted more funds for environmental protection from alternative sources. For example, Sectur allocated part of its tourism development budget for APA activities under its administration. Third, the involvement of several agencies sparked a competition to create and establish the institutional structure to administer APAs, since in so doing the agencies could enhance their political power and financial resources. Fourth, the participation of development agencies in this endeavor eased the resistance of local governments to state interference in land-use planning, constitutionally interpreted as a responsibility of local governments. Local governments were eager to attract investment in infrastructure, and the involvement of development agencies in APAs raised local expectations of state financial support.

In summary, to become a governmental priority in developing countries, strategies for environmental protection must be reconciled with economic development. Institutions in charge of development should be able to undertake initiatives in environmental protection. Innovative institutional arrangements must be in place to balance the sometimes conflicting objectives of development and environmental protection. Decentralization seems to be an alternative form of institutional arrangement. However, decentralization should not be conceived as simply a handover of responsibility and power to decentralized organizations. Central institutions must play a crucial role before, during, and after the decentralization process.

Two factors were important in explaining why horizontal decentralization at the state level enabled Bahia to achieve a certain degree of success in establishing APAs. First, although apparently unintentional, decentralization created a system of institutional incentives motivating development agencies to establish APAs. Protected areas were compatible with their development agenda based on nature-based tourism. Second, a system of checks and balances provided oversight for the whole process of development and environmental protection. Both APAs and some development projects needed the approval not only of the state environmental agency (CRA) but also of the state environmental council (CEPRAM), one third of whose members were from environmental groups.

The research findings led to some conceptual and policy lessons. First, policy process should be regarded as one whole process and not divided by stages (such as policymaking, policy implementation, and evaluation). Policymaking can be done effectively only if policy implementation is well understood and analyzed. The framework developed in Chapter 3 of this book can help analyze policy implementation. Second, the literature and practitioners often portray analytical frames in diametrically opposed choices: quantitative versus qualitative research, centralization versus decentralization, top-down versus bottom-up approaches. However, empirical studies have shown that a blending of approaches are necessary in practice and result in more effective policy implementation. The extremes hardly hold good results in practice. Finally, governments should make an effort to integrate environmental policies to the mainstream development policies by decentralizing policy implementation to development-oriented agencies. Environmental agencies should also move from the typical "policing" of other agents to work closely with other public and private actors to find out solutions to make compatible economic and social development with environmental protection.

Layout of the Following Chapters

Chapter 2 examines the relevant literature to understand the role of government in implementing environmental policies in developing countries. It starts with a debate concerning the dual mandate of governments: economic development and environmental protection. The chapter then introduces debates in the literature concerning institutional arrangements that enable governments to work more effectively. Finally, the main obstacles to implementing environmental policies in developing countries are identified.

Chapter 3 focuses on one of the main environmental management tools that governments can use to minimize the impacts of tourism development: protected areas. I describe the history of the different kinds of protected areas around the world. I also summarize the primary costs and benefits of establishing protected areas and how they are divided among stakeholders. After identifying the four main obstacles to implementing protected-area policy, particularly in developing countries, I then develop an analytical framework based on these four obstacles to apply to the Bahian case studies. This helps to explain how tourism has been a driven force for the establishment of protected areas around the world. The chapter ends by clarifying the general background needed for understanding the situation of protected areas in Brazil.

Chapter 4 analyzes the stories of the establishment of environmentally protected areas (APAs) in Bahia based on the analytical framework developed in Chapters 2 and 3. It investigates how the state of Bahia was able to establish a significant number of APAs with tourism potential in the 1990s by decentralizing APA policy to several state agencies. The involvement of various state agencies prompted them to increase their institutional capacity to handle this responsibility, and attracted funding and political support to both state and local levels. Finally, in Chapter 5 I summarize these results and frame more generally my contributions to planning and policy implementation.

2

The Implementation of Environmental Policies in Developing Countries

2.1 THE DUAL MANDATE OF GOVERNMENTS

Governments have a dual mandate in steering development. On the one hand, the low incomes and high poverty levels in many developing countries make economic development an important government objective. Government responsibilities include attracting private investment and spurring economic growth. Powerful ministries and agencies play a key role in determining interventions that shape economic development, including providing infrastructure, economic incentives, laws, and taxation, as well as creating policies, programs, and projects to pursue those priorities. On the other hand, governments are also responsible for environmental policy. One or various governmental agencies are expected to perform several actions in this arena, such as enacting and enforcing environmental laws, providing economic incentives for environmental initiatives, and controlling urban and land use planning.

These two government mandates—economic development and environmental protection—can be perceived as conflicting. Economic development can cause environmental degradation, and environmental protection can restrict economic development. Government agencies that oversee the two mandates, supported by allies in the private and

11

nongovernmental sector, can disagree over government action and clash in their attempts to gain political and institutional support.

Despite the increasing political support environmental issues have gained since the United Nations Conference on the Human Environment in Stockholm in 1972, the governments of many developing countries still perceive environmental protection as an obstacle to economic development. For example, in his study of several Caribbean countries, Gamman (1995) found in many cases that governments overturned environmental initiatives to support development projects. Influential private interests could convince government officials to approve their projects despite the concerns raised by environmental groups outside and inside the government.

What's more, while development agencies tend to maintain strong political connections and receive significant institutional and financial resources, environmental agencies often have few resources and little political clout. This is the case in several Eastern European countries. During the communist era environmental agencies had little influence in party politics and their officials could not promote many environmental initiatives (Klarer & Francis, 1997). Even with the collapse of communist regimes, environmental agencies remained in a fragile institutional position compared with development agencies. Economic recovery and attaining parity with Western Europe were the priorities.

The idea that governments could play a major role in environmental protection took hold in the 1960s and 1970s with growing pressure from environmental groups, first in industrialized countries and then in the developing world. At that time, economic development appeared to be one of the main villains of environmental quality. Theories promoting zero economic growth and highlighting the incompatibility of economic development and environmental protection were common. Facing public outcry, governments introduced new environmental laws and policies and created specialized agencies to implement them. These agencies, which often acted by policing and penalizing environmental offenders, were frequently blamed for blocking economic development and interfering with privacy and private property rights (Anderson & Leal, 1992).

However, in the 1980s the concept of sustainable development challenged the idea that environmental protection and economic development were incompatible. This concept holds that economic development and environmental protection go hand in hand, and governmental and private development actors began to think about how to integrate both objectives. Since then, numerous policies, procedures, and projects have focused on sustainable development trying to link social, environmental, and economic concerns (Villamor, 2006). However, although today it is difficult for countries, regions, and localities to consider any development action without also considering its environmental consequences and vice versa, the fields continue to exist independently (Brandon & Brandon, 1992). Government bureaucracies typically assign these responsibilities to different agencies or departments. As a result, environmental and developmental agencies interact with government policies, programs, and projects only when procedural steps are established, such as a requirement that an environmental agency analyze the impact of or approve development projects. Even when discourses are in tune, as in the case of sustainable development, agencies can disagree on everything from the nature and design of interventions to who implements them. Compatibility between development and environmental goals continues to be mostly a theoretical dream (Puppim de Oliveira, 2002).

Economic theory postulates that one way to make environmental and developmental objectives compatible is to put a price on environmental goods and quality (Anderson & Leal, 1992). Environmental value could then be aggregated with other economic values, and optimal economic solutions would be maximized. This approach implies that environmental goods are protected only when individuals and organizations (that is, the marketplace) value them. One extension of this idea is the environmental Kuznets curve, which plots the connection between changes in environmental quality and income. In the early stages of development, countries and regions increase their income while degrading the environment. As income reaches a certain level, environmental quality begins to improve as people place a higher value on it and have more income to devote to preserving it. For developing countries, the only way to attain high environmental quality is to become rich enough to afford environmental "goods" (Beckerman, 1992). The only role for governments in this context would be to value the cost of environmental degradation (Uhlig, 1992), to ensure that the market worked perfectly.

However, this approach has several limitations, even apart from the imperfect competition and asymmetry of information commonly ascribed to neoclassical economics. First, though environmental economics has evolved, it is difficult to place a value on environmental goods.

Second, although some environmental problems such as certain kinds of water and air pollution can be reversed, many losses such as extinct species are irreversible. The Kuznets curve does not suggest solutions for the latter. Also, some environmental issues do not seem to follow the curve, such as carbon emissions. Third, the development path is not the same in all localities; some regions may not have to degrade the environment at all to reach economic prosperity. Finally, the economic approach does not account for the fact that the benefits and losses of environmental degradation and economic development are not distributed evenly, generating conflicts. Moreover, economics has several limitations to deal with future generations. Thus, governments have more roles to play by steering development.

2.2. ORGANIZING THE STATE: CENTRALIZATION VERSUS DECENTRALIZATION

The distribution of government responsibilities and resources fundamentally shapes the interaction between economic development and environmental policy. Decentralization has been at the core of the development and governance debates in developing countries since the 1970s. These debates have focused on which levels of government should be involved in development, as well as to what extent. Estimates showed that decentralization was occurring in over 80 percent of developing and former communist countries in the end of the 1990s (Manor, 1999). A growing academic literature has focused on the political economy of decentralization (Manor, 1999; Souza, 1996; Bennet, 1990; Rondinelli & Cheema, 1983).

The growing interest in decentralized government policymaking and administration results from four main factors (Rondinelli & Cheema, 1983). First, extremely centralized development projects organized by huge and inefficient government bureaucracies in the 1950s and 1960s produced disappointing outcomes, sometimes even aggravating the problems they were supposed to tackle and creating social and environmental distress (Lutzenberger, 1985). Second, growth-with-equity development strategies of the 1970s called for popular participation in the development process. Third, expanding government services in an increasingly complex society were difficult to administer in a centralized manner. Finally, calls from international organizations as well as local civil society for greater democratization, accountability, and transparency in the 1980s and 1990s helped put decentralization at the core of the development debate.

A growing body of literature produced the theoretical rationale supporting decentralization. Proponents generated a long list of reasons why governments in developing countries should decentralize (Rondinelli, 1981; Rondinelli & Cheema, 1983). The main arguments can be summarized by two points. First, decentralization boosts government responsiveness to the needs and desires of citizens. Second, decentralization improves government efficiency and efficacy. Responding to social and political pressure, decentralized governments find ways to offer more efficient services.

The literature describes various ways for decentralizing governmental responsibilities. The most common approaches include deconcentration, delegation, devolution, and privatization (Rondinelli, 1981).[1] Deconcentration implies the transfer of tasks in a government agency from central offices (generally located in the capital) to offices located closer to the served population. These local offices are not politically independent or accountable to the local population but depend on the central government for budgets, instructions, and decision making. Delegation, in contrast, involves decentralizing tasks from the central government to other public organizations such as special function agencies or public corporations. Devolution entails the complete transfer of decisions regarding certain public responsibilities from a central government to a lower level government. Devolution for many authors captures the real spirit of decentralization, which is the transfer of authority to public institutions closer to the population (Parry, 1997). Finally, privatization, considered a form of decentralization by some authors, transfers certain public services from public to private organizations (Manor, 1999).

Decentralization has become a buzzword in development discourse—one that rhymes with democracy and efficiency. However, despite good intentions, these benefits often fail to materialize (Ribot et al, 2006; Parry, 1997; Ayee, 1994). Instead of generating more participatory local government, decentralization can simply allow local elites to control services and resources, creating a local autocracy. Instead of becoming more efficient through the use of local knowledge, services decline in quality owing to a lack of local institutional and technical capacity to perform the new tasks.

To produce the benefits that theory predicts, decentralization must do more than transfer authority and responsibility from one institution to another. The new institutions must develop the professional capacity, financial resources, and political support to deliver the services effectively.

National politicians and bureaucrats, afraid of losing power, can sabo-tage decentralization. Moreover, some authors suggest that central gov-ernments must play fundamental roles even when they decentralize power (Tendler, 1997). These roles range from developing the institu-tional capacity of local governments to monitoring and evaluating decentralized activities. Central governments must also prepare for this new role. Thus decentralization requires capacity building and political negotiation at all levels of government (Rondinelli & Nellis, 1986).

In developing countries, government policies tend to be viewed as highly centralized (Manor, 1999; Rondinelli and Cheema, 1983; Bennet, 1990; Morell & Poznanski, 1985). One agency or department is respon-sible for implementing a given policy and becomes jealous if other agencies interfere with its turf. Excessive centralization has been blamed for many policy failures in the past, and decentralization is viewed as a possible solution to these problems because different agencies are assigned complementary parts of a complex task. In the case of a tourism devel-opment project within an environmentally protected area, for example, an agriculture agency might spearhead reforestation, a tourism agency would attract private investment, an environmental agency would moni-tor resource use, a local municipality would develop a land-use master plan, and a transportation agency would build roads. However, in practice, the lack of coordination can doom such efforts, especially when agencies have different objectives and institutional capacities.

2.3 IMPLEMENTING PUBLIC POLICIES

Many people view policymaking as a matter of passing legislation, making plans, and distributing responsibilities. However, reality has taught a different story. Policies, programs, and projects often fail to be imple-mented as planned or exert unexpected impacts. The catastrophic con-sequences of massive development in the Brazilian Amazon in the 1970s are examples of this mismatch between policy conception and implementation (Moran, 1983; Lutzenberger, 1985).

Because scholars have often viewed implementation as secondary to policymaking, the political science literature often focuses on legis-lative and administrative processes: how issues arrive on the political agenda, how laws are approved, and how agencies are created. A schol-arly breakthrough occurred in 1973 with the release of *Implementation* by Jeffrey Pressman and Aaron Wildavsky. That book analyzed how a

U.S. program for helping minorities economically, led by the newly established Economic Development Administration (EDA), failed utterly, despite great expectations and much effort in Washington. In writing their book, the authors were surprised to discover a scarcity of serious academic attention to policy implementation, though they had heard so much about it. Pressman and Wildavsky's work awakened scholars to the promising but neglected field of implementation. The ensuing decade saw the publication of many works on both theory and practice (e.g., Rein & Rabinovitz, 1977; Bardach, 1977; Berman, 1978; Elmore, 1979). Debates over implementation became part of the scholarly agenda. However, more than three decades since the publication of Pressman and Wildavsky's influential work, disagreement remains over the basic definition of implementation, as well as the techniques for studying and modeling it (Najam, 1995).

Defining implementation is not an easy task. Scholars have used several definitions, from concise and simple to more elaborate ones. Rein and Rabinovitz (1977) define the "politics of implementation"— how policies change as they move from administrative guidelines into practice—as: "1) a declaration of government preferences, 2) mediated by a number of actors who 3) create a circular process characterized by reciprocal power relations and negotiations." Mazmanian and Sabatier (1983) present implementation as the "events and activities that occur after the issuing of authoritative public policy directives, which include both the effort to administer and the substantive impact on people and events." The study of implementation "requires understanding that apparently simple sequences of events depend on complex chains of reciprocal interactions" (Pressman & Wildavsky, 1973).

Some authors divide the implementation literature into generations (Goggin et al., 1990; Najam, 1995). Goggin et al. point to research in the 1970s that called attention to the need for an implementation research agenda. Although first-generation research demonstrated the complexities of implementation, such studies were accused of being case-specific, lacking theoretical grounding, overlooking cumulative knowledge, and emphasizing pessimistic views (Goggin et al., 1990). The second-generation studies tried to build theories on a larger number of case studies and develop models to explain variables and causality in implementation (Mazmanian & Sabatier, 1983; Van Meter & Van Horn, 1975). However, none of the models were able to validate propositions from earlier frameworks or replicate them in different cases.

Third-generation research tried to combine theoretical and empirical work to identify the key variables explaining why implementation works in some cases and fails in others (Goggin et al., 1990; Najam, 1995; Grindle, 1980). This approach continues today, with new approaches focusing on "success" cases in developing countries (Grindle, 1998; Tendler, 1997; Puppim de Oliviera, 2002).

Implementation has generated heated debates and various schools of thought. One of the most interesting concerns the top-down versus bottom-up approaches to implementing policy. Adherents of the former approach regard implementation as beginning with an authoritative decision, and assume that the process can be controlled from the top (Mazmanian & Sabatier, 1983; Van Meter and Van Horn, 1975). Countering this rationale, some scholars developed a bottom-up approach, in which street-level bureaucrats and the affected population greatly influence policy implementation (Elmore, 1979; Lipsky, 1980; Kaufman, 1973). Some of this research suggests that bottom-up influence not only occurs but is desirable because it adapts policies to local needs (Palumbo & Harder, 1981). These ideas coincided with the early boom in the decentralization literature (Rondinelli, 1981). Top-downers counterattacked, maintaining that bottom-uppers overemphasized the influence of local forces and that they failed to consider how best to implement policy (Sabatier, 1986). As the top-down versus bottom-up debate evolved, thinking converged: scholars realized that they needed to understand both influences.

Although some authors claim that their models based on developed countries are valid in any context (Van Meter & Van Horn, 1975), discussions of policy implementation have taken a different tack in developing countries. This discussion has occasionally been influenced by the debate in developed countries and vice versa (see Grindle, 1980). The discussion regarding developing countries has tended to be separate because of the assumption—never tested—that the implementation process and local conditions are substantially different than in developed countries. The literature on developing countries differs in three ways (Najam, 1995). First, it has been more case based and less dependent on models because of the greater diversity in social, cultural, and political contexts in these countries. Second, the case approach grounds this literature more firmly in the bottom-up approach. Finally, developing countries supposedly face more financial, technical, political, and cultural obstacles to implementing policy and tend to have "strong societies and weak states" (Migdal, 1988, quoted in Najam, 1995).

Emphasis on implementation in developing countries has shifted from "nothing works" case studies to "success cases" or best practices (Mahanty, 2002; Grindle, 1998; Tendler, 1997). The latter try to understand why a policy works even in a seemingly unfavorable context. These cases facilitate the understanding and design of policies in the same region or country or in countries with similar social and political contexts (Tendler, 1997). Evaluation professionals have also highlighted the importance of evaluating good practices to improve policy implementation in developing countries (Picciotto, 2003).

2.4 IMPLEMENTING ENVIRONMENTAL POLICY IN DEVELOPING COUNTRIES

The view of many developing countries regarding environmental protection changed significantly between the UN conference on the human environment held in Stockholm in 1972 and the Earth Summit held in Rio in 1992. In 1972, a group of developing countries stated that they would not sacrifice their economic development to protect the environment. In 1992, those countries came with a more progressive agenda, and many signed environmental treaties, leaving some developed countries (including the United States) on the defensive. However, implementation of environmental treaties such as those signed at Rio is left to individual countries, which must translate them into policies, programs, and projects to obtain results at national, regional, and local levels. At the point where intention becomes action several problems arise, making implementation a strenuous task; more often than not, environmental policies fail in developing countries. Shortages of technical capacity and scientific understanding may be one reason, but the complexity of the political economy in which the problem must be solved seems to exert an even stronger effect (Desai, 1992).

Environmental problems in developing countries come from two fundamental sources. On the one hand, problems result when a nation grows economically and embraces more affluent (or "modern") lifestyles. In those situations industrializing countries produce waste and use natural resources at almost the same pace as industrialized countries. On the other hand, environmental problems are rooted in the poverty that affects large segments of the population. Peasants use slash–and–burn agriculture in an unsustainable way for survival, causing deforestation (Pichon, 1992). Pastures are overgrazed, expanding desertification. A

lack of economic growth—and distribution of this growth—can per-
petuate or aggravate some of these problems (Quintana and Morse,
2005; Desai, 1992; World Bank, 1992).

The literature documents numerous failures in implementing
environmental policies in some developing countries, such as India
(Mahanty, 2002; Vyas & Reddy, 1998; Reich & Bowonder, 1992), China
(Ross, 1992; Jan, 1995), Eastern Europe (Prazan, Ratinger & Krumalova,
2005; Hardi, 1992; Klarer & Francis, 1997), and Latin America (Eastmond
& Faust, 2006; Pichon, 1992). Common explanations for policy failure
range from the classic Malthusian paradigm regarding rapid population
growth to widespread corruption in political systems (Shams, 1995).
Although these explanations may often be true, they do not suggest
practical solutions to problems in implementing environmental policies
in developing countries. To be useful to policymakers, analyses must
identify the main factors that impede successful implementation and
suggest how these obstacles could be overcome.

Toward that end, understanding the political economy in which
the implementation process occurs is crucial. As Pressman and Wildavsky
recognized, implementation—especially with regard to environmental
policy—encompasses the governmental and nongovernmental sector as
well as interorganizational links (1973). Thus, scholars have begun to
analyze what are the main forces driving changes in environmental
policy (Desai, 1998; Kamieniecki, 1993; Kamieniecki, Gonzalez & Vos,
1997) and how organizations work together to successfully implement
environmental policy in developing countries (Mahanty, 2002;
Brinkerhoff, 1996; Lopes et al., 1996; Lemos, 1998; Lemos & Oliveira,
2004). This literature provides practical recommendations to policymakers
in developing countries.

The literature on environmental policy has identified several obstacles to policy implementation. One branch of the literature, mostly by
economists, argues that distorted markets are the cause of most environmental problems or that market mechanisms can prove fundamental in
tackling environmental problems, even in developing countries (Panayotou,
1993; Anderson & Leal, 1992; Pearce & Turner, 1990). However, although
market mechanisms may have a role in encouraging environmental protection, I doubt that governments that fail to create institutions to implement other kinds of policies would succeed in creating the needed
market institutions and mechanisms. Most implementation problems are
institutional. These problems range from the lack of political support at

different levels of governments and of financial resources to the lack of institutional capacity (Puppim de Oliveira, 2002, 2005a).

First, environmental policies fail during implementation because they do not evoke enough political support from government or civil society at the central level, the local level, or both. This happens even in developed countries (Deroubaix & Leveque, 2005). Political support is essential in pressuring government agencies to enforce environmental legislation and counter the forces opposing environmental standards (such as groups of industrialists and farmers). The lack of political support for environmental enforcement is due primarily to the urgent need for economic development in developing countries. Widespread poverty and low incomes prompt governments to promote rapid industrialization and agricultural production that often causes environmental harm, as in India and China (Vyas & Reddy, 1998; Ross, 1992). In other countries, such as Indonesia, economic activities based on natural resources (mainly forestry and mining) are important sources of hard currency, convincing governments to promote or allow rapid exploitation, especially during economic crises (Boardman & Shaw, 1995). Environmental concerns, which often conflict with these kinds of economic activities, have no place on the agenda.

Moreover, environmental agencies, when they exist, are often politically weak and cannot oppose economic development interests. At the same time, civil society does not press governments and private actors to uphold environmental standards. Groups in civil society, such as environmentalists and neighborhood associations, were fundamental to the "environmental revolution" in developed countries, but they still are nonexistent or lack political clout in many developing countries. Although there are several normative arguments and practical reasons to stress the importance of participation by local actors in public policy making and implementation (Friedmann, 1973; Goulet, 1989; Healey, 1992; Hibbart & Lurie, 2000), action by civil society is hampered by political regimes, as in China (Ross, 1992; Jan, 1992) and Africa (Ylhaisi, 2003), or simply the lack of interest on the part of most of the population (Arjunan et al., 2006, Mahanty, 2002; Vyas & Reddy, 1998; USAID, 1979). Therefore, even though interest in participating in the planning process has grown in the last decades, particularly as it can influence policy outcomes in various ways (Angotti, 2000; Beard, 2002), a lot of obstacles prevent it from playing an important role in policy implementation in many countries (Puppim de Oliveira, 2005a).

However, with the democratization of many developing countries in the 1980s and 1990s, community and environmental groups have increasingly been in the vanguard pressing for better environmental standards and enforcement. Sometimes nongovernmental groups ally with progressive government and private actors to push for change. For example, in the Cubatao region of Brazil, one of the most polluted places in the world in the 1970s (called Death Valley), community groups, allied with officials in the state environmental agency, compelled polluting industries to comply with environmental regulations (Lemos, 1998).

Second, the main obstacle to implementing environmental policies, especially for poor governments in a country, region, or municipality, may be funding. "The commitment of these countries [in eastern and southern Africa] to sustainable environmental management is beset more by their lack of resources than by a lack of knowledge about the environment or lack of political will to promote sustainable development" (Salih, 1999). Developing countries may sometimes prioritize certain environment issues and obtain technical assistance to create elaborate plans, but the government may not have the financial resources to implement them in a sustainable manner. Although international donors sometimes provide funding, this financing usually covers a limited period of time and requires matching funds from governments, which are hard to obtain.

Finally, institutional capacity can be another obstacle to policy implementation. Besides the aforementioned lack of human resources, expertise, and equipment, institutional complexity can prove to be a major limitation. For example, some authors argue that decision making on environmental issues is too centralized and should be decentralized to local institutions (Desai, 1991). However, conflicts or lack of communication among agencies or levels of government complicate this process (Puppim de Oliveira & Ogata, 1998; Brinkerhoff, 1996; Vyas & Reddy, 1998). Others blame failure to implement policy on inadequate state-society relations and internal state organization, such as in Greece (Stevis, 1992). For Gamman (1995), the misunderstanding of the role of local culture by policymakers is one of the factors that can explain the nonimplementation of environmental policies in some Caribbean countries. Powerful ministries and pressing policies—perhaps as a result of a crisis—often divert resources from weak ministries or unpressing policies through official (budget discussions) or unofficial (behind-the-scenes political bargaining) means.

These obstacles (political, financial, and institutional) provide a framework for understanding policy implementation in developing countries. Investigating the institutional arrangements that can overcome such obstacles is the object of this book. For example, decentralization of policy implementation was the fundamental institutional arrangement that generated a large number of environmentally protected areas (APAs) in Bahia. The conditions under which this decentralization occurred placed protected areas in the mainstream development agenda of the state. As we will see in the following chapters, decentralization can create an institutional synergy that brings political, financial, and institutional support for APA policy at the state and local level. Chapter 3 analyzes the implementation obstacles for protected area policies and creates an analytical framework. Chapter 4 gives empirical evidence using the case study of Bahia, Brazil.

3

Obstacles to Policy
Implementation in the
Creation of Protected Areas

In order to analyze environmental policy implementation, this chapter discusses the establishment of protected areas around the world, particularly in Brazil. It looks at how the concept of protected areas evolved over time, from exclusive reserves for privileged groups to the "modern" conception of national parks like Yellowstone. The chapter also looks at how this conception often conflicts with the interests of the people who live within protected areas, especially in developing countries. The benefits and costs of protected areas are discussed, including how tourism has become an incentive to creating protected areas. This chapter then examines the four obstacles that can explain the failure of efforts to establish protected areas in many situations: lack of political support, lack of funding, lack of institutional capacity, and lack of support at the local level. From these four obstacles, I construct the analytical framework for the case studies used in this research.

3.1 A SHORT HISTORY OF THE EVOLUTION OF THE CONCEPT OF PROTECTED AREAS

A protected area can be defined as "an area dedicated primarily to the protection and enjoyment of natural or cultural heritage, to maintenance

25

of biodiversity, and/or to maintenance of ecological life-support services" (IUCN, 1991, quoted in Ceballos-Lascurain, 1996). For centuries, nations have created protected areas for different reasons, such as recreation, religion, and animal preservation. The first documented versions of protected areas appeared in China and India (Ceballos-Lascurain, 1996). As early as the 12 century B.C.E., Chinese rulers issued a decree for preserving forests. In 252 B.C.E., an Indian ruler circulated an edict protecting animals and forests. Pre-Colombian Mexico and African kingdoms also created different kinds of protected areas. Aztecs maintained zoological parks and botanical gardens. Rwandan rulers in precolonial times set aside certain areas where only part of the population had hunting rights.

In Western Europe, a comprehensive approach to creating protected areas appeared in the Middle Ages. At that time, the populations of game animals were declining in many locations owing to growing human population density, a greater number of hunters, and more efficient hunting methods. Nobles started worrying about the scarcity of prey. In 1084, William the Conqueror prepared an inventory of the natural resources of England, including forests and fishing and hunting reserves (MacKinnon et al., 1986). The first documented game reserve in Europe was established in Venice in the eighth century, when the local government set aside a natural refuge for boars and deer. The idea spread throughout Europe.

In the 19th century, industrialization and urban and agricultural expansion caused many environmental problems including water pollution and soil erosion. Natural areas where the growing population could seek recreation became scarce in the main urban centers. Wilderness advocates demanded the preservation of natural spaces for many reasons, including the preservation of watersheds, recreation, and human contact with nature. The American philosopher Henry Thoreau argued that wilderness was fundamental to the success of individuals and societies (Runte, 1997). In the United States, several efforts were made to create urban parks for providing leisure to urban dwellers, such as Central Park in New York and the Boston Commons. Around the same time, the American federal government also granted a piece of land to the state of California for creating Yosemite Valley State Park, the first legislation protecting scenic and recreational area for public use (Nash, 1978).

The turning point in the modern concept of environmentally protected areas was the establishment of the 3,000-square-mile Yellowstone National Park in the United States in 1872 (Dubasak, 1990). The first national park in the world, Yellowstone established a large-scale wilderness reserve in the public interest (Nash, 1978). Before Yellowstone, large protected areas had been created mostly for the enjoyment of upper-class elites. The creation of these private areas protected their abundance and aesthetic beauty from incursion by the majority of the population. Guards and wardens were used to enforce trespassing rules. Trespassers could receive severe punishment, including the death penalty (Nash, 1978). Yellowstone and Yosemite changed this concept, showing that public institutions could create large-scale protected areas for the purpose of preserving natural resources in the public domain. Another important milestone was the creation of Adirondack Park in New York, first as a forest preserve in 1885 and then as state park in 1892. In contrast to national parks, Adirondack State Park encompassed mostly private land. In this case the state government's reason for creating the park was the protection of watersheds that provided the public water supply for New York. This was achieved by restraining private development in a large area.

For over a century the spirit motivating Yellowstone has inspired the creation of protected areas for recreational, scenic, and economic values throughout the United States and many other countries, including Brazil (Padua, 1987). The Yellowstone Park Act provided a model for these efforts. That spirit was resurrected by the United Nations (UN) Conference on the Human Environment in Stockholm in 1972 and the tremendous growth of the environmental movement starting in the 1960s, first in developed nations and later in developing countries (Ceballos-Lascurain, 1996). As a result, protected areas grew significantly in the last three decades. During the 1970s, the number of such areas increased by 46 percent and their area by over 80 percent (Harrison et al., 1984). Many of these areas are in developing nations (MacKinnon et al., 1986). In 2003, there were more than 102,000 protected areas around the world covering 18.8 million km^2, about 11.5% of the Earth's land surface (IUCN & UNEP, 2003).

However, as the establishment of protected areas grew in developing countries, they often conflicted with the interests of local communities. The initial idea that protected areas were incompatible with human

activities was challenged. Conservation of nature and humans could not
be separated as in the design of the first parks (Diegues, 1994; Homewood,
2004). Moreover, another problem is that many rules for effective implementation of protected areas have not been enforced. Local support was
fundamental to implement protected area policy, as discussed below.

3.2 CATEGORIES OF PROTECTED AREAS

The modern concept of protected areas has evolved for more than a
century, and justifications for establishing protected areas have multiplied. From Yellowstone's principle of conserving wilderness for public
recreation, rationales have expanded to include preserving biodiversity,
pursuing scientific research, reproducing fauna and flora, maintaining
cultural values, developing tourism, using resources sustainably, and even
land-use planning. In this evolution, protected areas have assumed different forms to accommodate different objectives and managerial structures. Although national parks are the most common kind of protected
area in the world (Ceballos-Lascurain, 1996), many other categories of
protected areas have also become common.

    According to the World Conservation Union (IUCN), protected
areas can be divided into six categories (IUCN & UNEP, 2003; see
Table 3.1). The first category, strict nature reserves, limit human visita-
tion to scientific purposes. In general, these reserves include sensitive
ecosystems with rare or endangered species that cannot withstand even
minimal disturbances. The second category, national parks, is designed
to reserve natural areas encompassing important ecosystems for recreation. Human activities are limited to certain areas and intensities. Natural
monuments protect significant geological, biological, cultural, or aesthetic areas. Habitat management areas safeguard endangered fauna
and flora and include sites important for the reproduction and migra-
tion of species. Human presence is restricted to researchers and environmental restoration personnel. Protected landscape and seascape
sites are conceived to prevent significant changes in places with important aesthetic values. The last category, managed resource protected
areas, allows the sustainable use of natural ecosystems according to
community needs. This range of categories gives governments flexibility
in responding to the political, economic, social, and environmental
conditions at stake. The APAs in this book correspond to a mix of the
last two kinds of categories.

Table 3.1 Categories of Protected Areas

Category of Protected Area	Main Objective of Management
I. Strict nature reserve or wilderness area	For science and wilderness protection
II. National park	For ecosystem protection and recreation
III. Natural monument	For preservation of specific natural feature of inherent rarity, aesthetic or cultural significance
IV. Habitat or species management area	For conservation through management intervention to preserve threatened species
V. Protected landscape or seascape sites	For landscape/seascape conservation and recreation
VI. Managed resource protected area	For sustainable use of natural ecosystems according to community needs

Source: Adapted from IUCN & UNEP, 2003, p. 12.

3.3 COSTS AND BENEFITS OF PROTECTED AREAS

The establishment of protected areas implies costs and benefits for society. These can be distributed locally, regionally, or globally, and exert impacts over the short, medium, and long term. For example, a protected area can provide food for the local population, offer recreation for urban dwellers, and preserve genetic diversity. However, the costs and benefits of establishing protected areas are not distributed evenly among the parties involved. Creating protected areas often provokes conflicts over the uses of natural and cultural resources among different stakeholders.

Humans can benefit from conserving their natural environment, which supplies several kinds of services (Munasinghe, 1996; Ceballos-Lascurain, 1996; MacKinnon et al., 1986). The environment provides products that humans consume directly, including fish, fruit, and game animals. These products can be used by locals or commercialized. Many indigenous groups still subsist completely on forest products, and rural residents often depend on the products they gather from surrounding natural environments. Other local populations collect and sell natural products to acquire cash. Some do that in sustainable ways—including traditional fishing communities and rubber tappers—and others in unsustainable ways—such as giant logging companies in tropical zones.

Moreover, the environment can absorb and transform some of the byproducts of human activity, such as sewage and carbon dioxide. For example, forests hold a significant fraction of the greenhouse gases. Nature also maintains numerous life-support systems, such as watersheds supplying urban areas. The natural environment helps control local natural disasters; floods, landslides, and siltation can be mitigated by environmental protection. Human-induced changes in regional and global environments, meanwhile, could destabilize sea currents and climate, causing droughts and floods of catastrophic proportions.

The environment also contains an uncountable pool of genes whose characteristics are still poorly assessed, perhaps containing medical or nutritional properties. In addition, humans use the natural environment for recreation; a growing number of people practice ecotourism in their leisure time. Recreation can create economic activities that generate jobs and income.

Despite these benefits, several costs are implied in the establishment of any environmentally protected area—costs that are usually shared by governments and the local population. First, preliminary studies, including scientific assessments and negotiations with local governments and people, are needed to determine the viability and importance of the proposed area. Second, once the area is created, it will need a management plan. For example, large parts of the forest around the world lack management plans (Siry, Cubbage, & Ahmed, 2005). This work can be performed totally or partially by the institution in charge of the area or by hired consultants. If this process involves local participation, organizing the participatory process will impose added costs. In the case of environmentally protected areas (APAs) in Bahia, these costs vary from US$ 40,000 to $250,000 for each APA, depending on the characteristics of the area, according to the technical staff of government.

Third, many protected areas include private lands, and governments must expropriate the areas and compensate private landowners. The costs of doing so can be considerable, especially if large portions of the protected areas are private. For instance, nearly all of the Monte Pascoal National Park in Bahia was under private ownership when it was created in the 1960s (WWF, 1994). In the first Brazilian national park (Itatiaia, created in 1937), construction projects continue inside the park because landowners have not been compensated yet. The costs of compensation can escalate if landowners fight in court for more money. Governments in developing countries often struggle to find the financial resources to pay landowners, and many international donors to environmental projects like the World Bank do not provide funds for land acquisition (WWF, 1994).

Once a protected area is established, environmental restoration, monitoring, and enforcement require additional funds. Part-time or full-time personnel, private firms, and NGOs must be hired to operate and maintain protected areas. Enforcement officials need to be adequately equipped with vehicles (and fuel) and communication equipment; surveillance flights, computers, and satellite imagery are sometimes required for periodic surveys.

Indirect costs are also associated with the creation of protected areas. Governments lose taxes previously assessed to the land and on economic activities that would otherwise have occurred in the protected area. Governments must also sometimes compensate neighboring landowners for the damage to their property caused by wild animals from the protected area. Finally, there are the opportunity costs of locking up land and natural resources—the gains foregone from harvesting and selling resources and pursuing other economic activities such as agriculture or urban development.

3.4 THE FRAMEWORK FOR EXPLAINING FAILED EFFORTS TO ESTABLISH PROTECTED AREAS

With growing information about the potential benefits of protected areas and pressure from environmentalists, the number of such areas rose significantly during the last three decades, especially in developing countries (IUCN & UNEP, 2003; Ceballos-Lascurain, 1996). However, academics, policymakers, and environmentalists agree that the need to expand the number of protected areas in certain ecosystems even further is urgent—as is the need to improve their management structures (declaration of the last World Congresses on National Parks and Protected Areas in 1992 and 2003, in McNeely, 1993, 13–16; see also IUCN, 2003). While some governments in the developing world, such as Costa Rica, have pursued aggressive policies for establishing and maintaining protected areas effectively, many other countries have lagged in these efforts (Lu et al., 2003; Barzetti, 1993). Indeed, for every profitable and successful protected area, there may be hundreds that are not successful (Boo, 1990). In Brazil, the Iguaçu National Park is one of the few that generate revenues higher than the maintenance costs. Promoting, establishing, and implementing environmentally protected areas is not often a top priority in regions where poverty alleviation, rapid economic development, and resolution of internal and external conflicts are urgent needs. To succeed, protected areas must provide proven solutions to those needs instead of creating another set of problems.

Although the benefits of protected areas are enormous, several challenges to creating and implementing them must be confronted (Puppim de Oliveira, 2002). First, protected areas are rarely perceived as an urgent need and thus do not attract much political support. Moreover, they can generate conflicts with landholders. Second, once political obstacles to creating protected areas are overcome, governments often lack the funds to establish and manage them. Most environmentally protected areas in Latin America, for example, exist only on paper (Barzetti, 1993). Third, even when funding is not a problem, many government bureaucracies lack the institutional capacity to ensure effective implementation. For instance, even though national and international sources of funding were available, institutional "incapacity" was blamed for failures in implementing protected-area policies at the federal level in Brazil (WWF, 1994). Fourth and finally, local populations and governments often resist the establishment of protected areas because they see them as interfering in local matters and more of a burden than a benefit. These four obstacles are the basis of the framework to analyze implementation of environmental policies. I will discuss these four obstacles in detailed in the following sections.

3.4.1 Lack of Political Support

Protected areas need to generate substantial political support. Governmental and nongovernmental environmental groups trying to establish such areas have long faced strong opposition from private development interests and local populations, who see them as threats to economic activity or as government interference with private property (Nash, 1978). On the other hand, governments themselves often regard the creation of protected areas as a troublesome issue that should be avoided unless strong political or public pressure supports such an effort. Protected areas generally entail expropriation of private land, cessation of some economic activities (such as logging and construction), development restrictions, and interference with local matters. Such activities can generate controversy and opposition from strong political constituencies and lobbyists, including farmers, developers, property rights groups, and logging interests. Although these groups often do not constitute a local majority, they have financial resources and political contacts and can mobilize to inflict substantial political damage (Casson and Obidzinski, 2002). In some dictatorships, especially in developing countries, these groups control the government and can silence environmental interests. Moreover, governments must assign and justify the institutional and financial resources to create and implement a protected-area policy from a limited budget (often operating with a deficit). This situation has been aggravated in the last decade with growing international pressure on governments to cut their activities, deficits, and taxes.

Many of the political conflicts provoked by protected areas relate to the fact that different interests compete over the use of natural resources and land. Indeed, some authors point out that early national parks were created only because their land was *not* suitable for other uses, or there were no conflicting interests at stake (Nash, 1978; Pouliquen-Young, 1997). National parks such as the Grand Canyon, Yosemite, and Yellowstone were created in areas marginal for exploitation. No large park was created in highly productive agricultural regions, such as Illinois or Iowa (Nash, 1978). Similarly, in Brazil, all large national parks (with areas over 500,000 hectares) are basically in the Amazon region (WWF, 1994), mostly in remote areas where land has few competing uses and the creation of national parks is unlikely to cause conflicts.

When large natural areas were abundant, few people saw the need to set aside areas for environmental preservation. Environmental movements did not have the same political power they have today. In the United States, for example, the concepts of national parks and environmentalism were contrary to many powerful 19-century ideas regarding territorial expansion, conquest of nature, and exploitation of natural resources.

In industrialized countries, environmental movements grew to become an important political force propelling creation of protected areas and other environmental initiatives. However, especially in developing countries, the notion of environmental protection has seemed antagonistic to the need for rapid economic development to alleviate widespread poverty. At the UN Stockholm conference in 1972, the Brazilian government, together with other developing nations, positioned itself radically against the environmental agenda. That agenda was seen as a maneuver of the industrialized countries to impede developing nations from industrializing, and external interference in domestic matters (Loureiro & Pacheco, 1995). Thus, environmentalism was not, and still is not in many countries, an important political force mobilizing support for protected areas. Some progress in developing countries regarding protected areas was initiated by committed public officials or important personalities sympathetic to environmental causes. In Brazil, for example, an influential public administrator suggested creating the first national parks, and a public bureaucrat created a new class of protected areas that could be established without interference from pro-timber interests (Padua, 1987; Nogueira Neto, 1992). In Costa Rica, the government successfully adopted ecotourism as an economic alternative early on (Boo, 1990).

With the democratization of various developing countries, especially in Latin America, many environmental movements have emerged and begun trying to mobilize the population and influence political decision making. Public and government interest in environmental matters therefore seems to have grown (Siry, Cubbage, & Ahmed, 2005; Boo, 1990). However, many environmental groups in developing countries act only locally and do not have strong institutional or financial resources. Although sometimes these groups are numerous, they do not have the cohesion of other organized interest groups (especially those related to economic development) that promote their political agenda in the legislature and executive branch. Environmental interests within the government similarly often have little political power, so they are underfunded. They also lack the important political contacts of pro-development groups. For example, the head of an environmental agency in many developing countries is often a scientist or an environmentalist without many political contacts or the savvy to promote the agency's interests. Organizing these environmental constituencies and strengthening their ability to influence political decisions are essential if the number and size of protected areas are to grow, according to specialists and advocates worldwide (McNeely, 1993).

The lack of political support for protected areas is often attributed to deficient communication concerning the importance of such areas

(McNeely, 1993). The economic and social benefits of protected areas are numerous (Boo, 1990; Ceballos-Lascurain, 1996; Wells, 1997), but environmental interests sometimes lack the skills and resources to spread the word through environmental education, political lobbying, and the use of mass media. For example, the success of the U.S. National Park Service in building broad support for national parks was credited to the service's first director (Nash, 1978). An expert in public relations, this director placed articles about the parks in national magazines and brought key politicians to tour the protected areas. These activities enhanced public concern over protected areas and built broad political support for them within the federal government and Congress.

The recent rise of ecotourism has enabled policymakers and the public to perceive the benefits of protected areas, as tourism is a tangible direct benefit. This facilitates communication with and support from a broader constituency for protected areas. In Bahia, the state government mustered the support of many pro-development actors for protected areas by extensively advertising the ecotourism benefits (Bahia State Government, 1997).

The distribution of responsibility for protected areas within governments is also important in securing political and institutional support (MacKinnon et al., 1986). Placing protected areas within the jurisdiction of an underfunded and politically weak agency, such as the environment ministry in many developing countries, can undermine support. Some authors suggest that protected areas should be placed under the control of powerful revenue-generating agencies such as agriculture and forestry (MacKinnon et al., 1986). However, if environmental objectives clash with the primary goals of these development agencies, they could simply support the latter, neglecting environmentally protected areas (Puppim de Oliveira & Ogata, 1998).

Another issue in assigning government responsibility is whether all protected areas should be under the control of one agency. Such an approach could improve institutional coordination and assign full responsibility for success or failure to that agency. That approach would also unify pro-protection political activity, as the agency could be the bastion fighting for protected areas within government. External actors would know which officials to pressure in order to stimulate government action regarding protected areas. However, concentrating protected areas within one agency could also create a backlash. The agency might be viewed as the "environmental police," generating conflicts with and political isolation from other government bureaucracies and leaders. The agency could also be poorly managed, preventing significant action on protected areas. Although some authors support the place-ment of the agency in one politically strong and revenue-generating ministry or department (MacKinnon et al., 1986), strong ministries or departments in developing countries are often under budgetary con-straints and give protected areas low priority. Protected-area policy may also clash with the developmental priorities of a more powerful min-istry, such as the expansion of agricultural or timber production.

Decentralization of responsibility for protected areas among sev-eral agencies could produce a governmental coalition supporting envi-ronmentally protected areas. These agencies could work together to gain approval for their projects. However, decentralization could also spur competition and grievances among the agencies, spurring them to block each other's projects. Decentralization could also open a political vacuum in which each agency hands responsibility to others and no agency assumes any real responsibility for protected areas (Puppim de Oliveira & Ogata, 1998).

There is no consensus or much empirical evidence on the best way to establish responsibility for protected areas within government institu-tions. Governments have adopted different approaches to assigning such responsibilities. In the United States, the federal government dispersed responsibility for protected areas among several agencies in different departments, mainly Interior, Agriculture, and Defense (U.S. Department of the Interior, 1975). In some countries, such as Uganda and Tanzania, protected areas assume a parastatal form that gives them more political independence from government (MacKinnon et al., 1986). In Brazil, since the 1980s, the federal government has concentrated responsibility for all federally protected areas in one agency, the Federal Environmental Agency (IBAMA, or Instituto Brasileiro do Meio Ambiente e dos Recursos Naturais Renováveis). At the state level, assignment of protected area responsibilities has varied. For example, in Bahia they were dispersed among several state agencies in different secretariats until the end of the 1990s, when they were concentrated in one agency.

3.4.2 Lack of Funding for Protected Areas

One of the major problems facing protected areas in developing coun-tries is a lack of funding (McNeely, 1993). In many countries, public institutions have limited financial resources even for the most basic public services, such as education and water supply. Some government services depend on external aid just to survive at a minimal level. Even in medium-income countries such as Brazil, some states and municipalities operate under precarious conditions and provide almost no public services. Environmental protection is rarely a priority on their political agendas. Moreover, in the last decade proponents of neoliberalism have argued that to compete in a global economy, governments must reduce their deficits and shrink their operations. To improve environmental management and establish new protected areas, public agencies often have to hire new people, invest in training and equipment, and expand their operating and maintenance capacity, but funds are scarce and hiring public employees is difficult in this climate. In Brazil, the federal environmental ministry received a mere 0.2 percent of the budget in the beginning of the 2000s (Puppim de Oliveira et al, 2002a).

Under such conditions, where can governments find the financial resources to maintain and expand protected areas? Many possible sources of funding for protected areas do exist. Those sources include government budgets, park entrance fees, taxes on products such as tobacco and alcohol, private and nonprofit groups, and international agencies (such as the Global Environmental Facility (GEF) and the U.S. Agency for International Development). These private, nonprofit, and international sources often fund specific projects, but the funds are also sporadic and temporary. Common sources of financing for protected areas are trust funds managed by a governmental or quasi-governmental institution. However, external sources generally make only a limited contribution to these funds, which governments must match with substantial resources, including personnel, material, services, and cash (MacKinnon et al., 1986). Thus, the bulk of sustainable funding for protected areas usually comes from internal sources, mainly entrance fees and government budgets, as in the case of Brazil.

Many protected areas generate substantial income from visitors. Some of these areas are profitable, with the surplus used to support other less profitable areas. In Rwanda, park entrances in the Parc National des Volcans earned approximately US$ 1 million per year before the civil war. In Ecuador, the Galapagos National Park generated US$ 700,000 per year in direct revenues (WTO & UNEP, 1992). In the United States, cost recovery from users ranged from under 10 percent for the national park system to more than 100 percent for New Hampshire state parks (LaPage, 1996). In South Africa, the government cut funds for maintaining protected areas, but operations contributed for almost half the areas' funding in 1995 (Wells, 1996). Federal and provincial governments in Canada collected US$ 1.7 billion annually in taxes from wildlife-related tourism, but spend only about US$ 300 million on those programs.

In some developing countries, the recovery rate from investments in wildlife conservation can be more than 5 to 1 (Ceballos-Lascurain, 1996). However, there are many cases where tourism revenues do not fulfill expectations and the protected-area system collapses from underfunding. In Benin, Africa, the revenues from tourism were much lower than expected—too low to adequately fund the park system or to provide income for the local population (Sayer, 1981, quoted in Boo, 1990). Several protected areas do not attract many visitors because they do not have important attractions or are located in remote areas with poor infrastructure. Therefore, in many developing countries, protected areas are not properly managed because there is not enough funding from entrance fees and governments cannot afford to support them.

In many countries, government budgets continued to finance the creation and management of protected areas either totally or partially (Mackinnon et al., 1986). Even where protected areas successfully raise capital from visitors, as does the U.S. National Park Service, government budgets must complement the funds for proper management (Nash, 1978). Agencies in charge of protected areas must fight for portions of the budget within a department or government. Those agencies must be technically convincing and politically skillful in their arguments to persuade budgetary administrators of the need for funding. Sometimes the relationship between costs and benefits of a protected-area system is not clear. Although preserving natural resources generates many social benefits, these are often indirect and nonmonetary in nature, spead out over time. Their value is difficult to account for precisely. Environmental agencies do not receive any real cash for those benefits.

Another challenge is that many of the costs of creating and implementing protected areas must be paid up front or over the short term. Environmental agencies must hire employees, buy land and material, and pay bills. Even though entrance and other fees can make some protected areas profitable, governments often lack the funds for upfront investments needed to establish protected areas to get the returns in the long run.

In short, the cost-benefit analysis often used in governmental decision making overlooks many benefits, even though techniques for evaluating those benefits have improved in the last two decades. Nev-

ertheless, it is difficult to promote intangible benefits within governments that are short of cash for investment and operating costs. Moreover, it is very difficult to maintain protected areas only with revenues
from them. Governments most likely need to complement the budget
from other funding sources.

3.4.3 Lack of Institutional Capacity

Political support and funding are essential for the establishment of
protected areas. A comprehensive protected-area policy requires the
endorsement of a strong political constituency to put it on the government agenda and to overcome opposing forces. It also needs funding for planning and implementation. However, even with political
support and funds, protected area policies can fail because many
governments have weak or no institutional capacity to carry out
policy objectives. Agencies in charge of protected areas may lack or
misuse personnel, training programs, and materials. In Madagascar,
lack of institutional capacity of the agencies in charge of protected
areas were one of the main obstacles to improving them (Hannah et
al., 1998). In Brazil, the Federal Environmental Agency (IBAMA)
attracted several national and international sources of funding for
protected areas, but it did not have the institutional capacity to implement a comprehensive policy (WWF, 1994). The misallocation of
personnel was one of the reasons for that. IBAMA had 7,000 employees, but only about 6 percent (437 employees) worked on protected
areas in the mid-1990s. As a result, IBAMA lagged in the implementation of many programs involving protected areas. For instance, the
National Fund for the Environment (FNMA, or Fundo Nacional do
Meio Ambiente) was created in 1989 and assigned US$ 22 million for
environmental protection between 1992 and 1996, thanks to a loan
from a development bank. However, only US$ 1.8 million had been
used by the end of 1993 because of institutional deadlocks.

Another impediment for effective policy implementation is corruption among government officials in charge of environmental protection. Environmental protection can affect economic interests and generate
opportunities for corruption between the public and private sector. For
example, 25 percent of the enforcement officials in the Brazilian Environmental Agency (IBAMA) were arrested by the Federal Police in
August 2006 due to involvement in a bribery scheme for helping to
procure environmental licences and overlooking violations. Therefore,

transparency and an independent monitoring and evaluation system for policy implementation is important to have better control of corruption.

To implement protected-area policies, government organizations need to perform several activities, including proposing and planning protected areas, developing management plans, gaining approval from legal and political authorities, as well as motivating the participation of the local population (Pinto da Silva, 2004; Agrawal and Gupta, 2005; MacKinnon et al., 1986; UNEP & WTO, 1992). These activities require a certain institutional capacity on the part of organizations in charge of protected areas. This institutional capacity may include qualified personnel (full- or part-time employees and consultants), infrastructure, appropriate equipment, and services. With this capacity in place, government organizations can perform studies, conduct field trips, negotiate with other actors, analyze consulting reports, respond to political demands, and publish material. If an adequate institutional capacity is not in place, organizations have to build a structure to implement a protected-area policy. To improve their capabilities, organizations may have to buy equipment and services, hire or move staff, contract with consultants, and invest in short-term or continuous training.

Protected-area policies should rest on an organizational structure that has, or can build, the institutional capacity to perform the implementation task properly. As we saw in a previous section, governments can place all protected areas under one governmental or parastatal organization. This can concentrate, instead of dispersing, efforts to acquire the skills, personnel, and resources for effective protected-area management while avoiding rivalries and the lack of coordination among different agencies (MacKinnon et al., 1986). However, overlapping the same governmental function among several agencies can generate synergistic effects (Landau, 1969). When more than one agency is working on the same problem, the chances that one of them will actually do the work increase. Also, agencies can cooperate to complement each other's efforts. For example, one agency might have more expertise in biological surveys, offering this service to other agencies; another might have officials more experienced in physical planning who can compensate for the lack of this know-how in other agencies. Individual agencies may also strive to improve their institutional capacity to gain leverage for protected-area projects. By working more efficiently and effectively, agencies can demand or create more projects and gain political prestige.

Several possible organizational arrangements could ensure adequate institutional capacity for implementing protected-area policies. From the literature, it appears that there is not enough evidence to suggest one right model. Effective implementation of such policies seems to depend on several factors, including initial institutional capacity in the government, funding alternatives, the relationship among participating agencies, the existence and attitude of nongovernmental actors, and opportunities for improving institutional capacity.

3.4.4 Lack of Cooperation and Coordination at the Local Level

The successful establishment of protected areas depends on the support of local governments and communities (Kaljonen, 2006; Gbadegesin and Ayileka, 2000; Ceballos-Lascurain, 1996; UNEP & WTO, 1992; Boo, 1990; MacKinnon et al., 1986). If locals perceive protected areas as interference in local matters or a burden, they can become uncooperative and make fulfilling protection objectives almost impossible (MacKinnon et al., 1986). However, locals can also play a key role in implementing protected-area objectives if they view them as beneficial in the short and long term (Albers & Grinspoon, 1997). Locals can provide important information for developing the management plan, and complement institutional capacity by helping publicize and enforce protected-area guidelines.

In many countries, local governments or communities determine land-use rules and legislation. When an upper-level government (such as the state or federal government) establishes protected areas, it is restricting land use. Such a move could conflict with local interests and the politicians who promote them. Although upper-level legislation regarding protected areas generally overrules local legislation, local governments are important in generating support for protected areas, as they know the key members in their communities. They can help inform the local population, and they are often knowledgeable about the main threats and problems at the local level.

To complement upper-level governmental action, local officials can pass their own legislation legitimizing protected areas and provide some institutional capacity to implement protected-area guidelines. However, governmental levels may dispute jurisdiction over land use or environmentally protected areas, and such disputes can compromise their implementation. For example, in South Africa, efforts to establish protected areas in some regions have failed because of conflicts between provincial wildlife conservation agencies and the national park board (Wells, 1996).

When the modern conservation movement began at the end of the 19th century, the notion of a protected area implied the complete removal of humans. These areas would be "islands" where nature would be left alone, separate from human activities except for those entailed in appreciating it. As the American conservation advocate John Muir said in 1890, "Our wild mountains should be saved from all sorts of commercialism and marks of man's work" (quoted in Nash, 1978). Protected areas were designed as a modern idealization of what nature should be, untouched by humans (Diegues, 1994), so policy prioritized "fortress conservation" (Homewood, 2004).

As the conservation movement expanded to developing countries, many protected areas were created regardless of the existence of local people. Often these people had lived in the region for generations, sometimes before formal states were established. Lines for parks or reserves were drawn without considering the fact that people lived in those areas or used them for cultural, religious, or subsistence activities, such as hunting, fishing, and collecting fruit and firewood (Rawat, 1997). In some cases, local populations were forced out. In many parts of Africa, police enforced protected areas at the expense of local people during the colonial era, and even after it had ended (Wells, 1996). In Brazil, indigenous people who had been living in the Monte Pascoal National Park before the Portuguese arrived in Brazil in 1500 were expelled and prohibited from entering the new park, confined instead to a reservation next to it.

In the last four decades, as many developing countries have expanded their protected areas, such moves have provoked local conflicts (Tisdell, 1995; Fiallo & Jacobson, 1995). Local communities have often borne great losses when protected areas have been established, and have gained almost no benefits (Wells, 1996). Policymakers, park managers, and academics have begun to realize that local people should benefit from protected areas and are fundamental to their design and implementation (Pinto da Silva, 2004; Mahanty, 2002; MacKinnon et al., 1986; McNeely, 1993; Ceballos-Lascurain, 1996; Albers & Grinspoon, 1997).

Local communities often use the natural resources that are the target of preservation (Straede and Treue, 2006). With the creation of protected areas, communities generally have to give up the use of those resources either totally or partially. If the area attracts tourists, communities have to share their natural resources and communal spaces (Ceballos-Lascurain, 1996). Thus, many communities may be uneasy or hostile to the idea of protected areas. To support them, communities need to feel that they are benefiting because their natural resources are protected from poachers or because they gain from tourism and other activities. In these cases, the local governments and communities perceive environmental assets are key to conservation efforts (Xu et al., 2006; Alessa, Bennett & Kliskey, 2003).

Officials implementing protected areas can compensate communities through several mechanisms. They include paying for land claims, sharing revenues from park entrance fees, employing local people, purchasing local goods, encouraging local participation in tourism enterprises, and offering development assistance to local projects (Wells, 1996).

Development projects compensate local populations for the opportunity costs of foregone activities in protected areas. Such projects can involve building roads, enhancing the water supply, providing sewage treatment, and constructing schools and hospitals. These projects also often improve the infrastructure for tourism activities, from which communities benefit indirectly as well. Local governments also gain politically from these projects, as politicians can claim credit for delivering them.

Of course, such projects can increase development pressures on protected areas and facilitate access to illegally harvested products such as timber and wild animals. Development projects like roads can also spur activities that can threaten protected areas, including agriculture, cattle raising, and new development. Thus, development efforts should rest on a detailed analysis of their benefits to local people and tourism versus their threats to conservation.

The possibility of benefiting economically and culturally from tourism can encourage local populations to support protected areas. With the growing market for ecotourism (Boo, 1990), locals have new income opportunities. Possibilities range from establishing their own businesses, to becoming guides, to selling their products, to working for new tourism business. Some countries, like Costa Rica, established successfully several ecotourism projects with substantial support from the local population (Boo, 1990). However, many ecotourism projects fail, frustrating the local population (Sayer, 1981). Locals sometimes invest a significant part of their savings, or even loans, in failed tourism enterprises. Also, tourism activities often mostly benefit outsiders, leaving the local population with only marginal jobs (Wilkinson, 1992).

Communication and training are major components of raising support for protected areas at the local level (Mahanty, 2002; MacKinnon et al., 1986; McNeely, 1993). Local populations may develop negative attitudes toward protected areas when they are not well informed about them (Fiallo & Jacobson, 1995). Locals should be aware of restrictions on protected areas, but most importantly, they should clearly associate environmental conservation with income opportunities (Straede & Treue, 2006). This can be achieved through public hearings, door-to-door contacts, local media, and environmental education in local schools.

To help locals benefit from tourism, they should receive training in tourism activities and information about and financing their own enterprises (Wells, 1996). Training and information can spur environmental consciousness and the establishment of local nongovernmental environmental groups. These groups could convince governments of the need to create local environmental agencies to help enforce protected-area guidelines. Training could also focus on building local institutional capacity to complement enforcement. The agency in charge of the protected area could provide training for local governments and NGOs in enforcing environmental rules. They could also hire them or provide equipment and personnel to perform some or all of the enforcement tasks.

The process of delineating protected areas is also an important factor in avoiding conflicts with local populations or governments (MacKinnon et al., 1986). From a conservation standpoint, biological preservation should be a priority; various models discuss the optimal shape of certain protected areas (Dearden, 1988). However, the limits of protected areas should also take into account several other factors, such as tourism needs, local government borders, local economic activities, and existing systems of land tenure.

Protected areas can include one or more local governments. Spreading a protected area over several governmental jurisdictions can avoid conflict because only part of a certain municipality or province is set aside for preservation. Such an approach can also encourage several governments to share enforcement. On the other hand, the involvement of several jurisdictions can make coordination difficult. Lack of communication, training difficulties, and local rivalries can compromise the success of the implementation task.

The flexibility and will to negotiate the use of natural resources and land with local landowners and communities are also significant factors. Sometimes negotiating less strict environmental rules with local actors can attract local support, but such support can also come at the cost of a smaller protected area and lower level of conservation (Albers & Grinspoon, 1997).

Protected-area authorities and locals could jointly define environmental guidelines and reach a formal or informal agreement balancing local and preservation interests. Locals could be allowed to harvest certain products from the protected area, such as fish or fruit. For example, local villagers supported the Sariska Tiger Reserve in India and Maputo Elephant Reserve in Mozambique, even though wild animals caused losses on their properties, because they were allowed to gather fodder, fuel wood, and other resources from these reserves (Sekhar, 1998; De Boer & Baquete, 1998). Landowners or communities could also be allowed to develop part of their land if they preserve the rest. Flexibility in land use and environmental rules can alleviate restrictions on locals, but the degree of flexibility and negotiation of those rules should depend on the kind of protected area, the initial local situation, and the willingness of locals to comply with agreements.

Analysis of the role of local actors in establishing and managing protected areas is complex. Moreover, pursuing effective local participation is not easy. Extensive experience in several countries demonstrates that active local participation in developing countries is rare and difficult to achieve (Wells, 1996; Puppim de Oliveira, 2005a). Varying social, economic, institutional, and environmental situations makes it difficult for one region to learn from the experiences of another. Widespread poverty in developing countries is a challenge and may restrict the goal of preservation. A balance between conservation, development, and human needs should be the goal of many protected areas in developing countries.

Overall, these four challenges—the lack of political support, lack of funding, lack of institutional capacity, and lack of support at the local level—supply the framework for analyzing the case studies in Bahia presented in Chapter 4. I discuss how the decentralization of a protected-area policy to several state agencies overcame each of the four obstacles at the state level, thanks to the growing presence of tourism in the region.

3.5 TOURISM AS A FORCE FOR ESTABLISHING PROTECTED AREAS

The natural environment has emerged as a competitive asset that brings tourists and investment to many regions of the world, generating economic development (Deng, King, & Bauer, 2002; Butler, 1991). However, the impacts of tourism development can destroy the same environment and undermine further investment (Briassoulis, 1995; May, 1991). Indeed, poor environmental management can ultimately destroy tourism itself.

Concern about the important role of the environment in supporting economic activity is not new. In the tourism field, these concerns started to appear in the 1970s when the environmental and social impacts of tourism on certain regions became more evident (Hunter & Green, 1995). Places like Acapulco in Mexico, the French Riviera, and Mallorca and Torremolinos in Spain faced environmental problems related to tourism (Bosselman, 1978, Llinas, 1996; Pollard and Rodriguez, 1993).

Governments play two central roles in developing tourism (Puppim de Oliveira, 2003). Public funds can be used to construct the necessary infrastructure and promote tourism. Government agencies in charge of environmental and land-use regulation must also control the social and environmental impacts of tourism. These two public roles may seem contradictory, but they do not need to be.

Governments often first concentrate their efforts on promoting tourism and then later, when environmental conditions deteriorate to levels that threaten tourist activity, try to mitigate tourism's impacts (Mathieson & Wall, 1996). However, since the mid-1980s, environmental quality has been deemed essential to the growth of tourism, and several governments have recognized the importance of this activity for economic development. Consumers as well as local and external actors have pressured governments to change their development approach. Thus, many governments are introducing tools for environmental planning and management to prevent environmental degradation from infrastructure projects.

These two government roles—development promoter and environmental protector—seem to inevitably conflict especially in developing countries where the pressure for rapid tourism development exists in pristine areas. On the one hand, critics have singled out government investment as one of the main causes of environmental degradation in many developing countries.[1] On the other hand, key leaders of developing countries claimed that they did not want to sacrifice economic development for environmental protection and that they did not have enough resources to invest in environmental quality.[2]

However, tourism seems to be a force of change on the environmental agenda for many governments in developing countries (Puppim de Oliveira, 2005). Tourism has the potential to become an important economic activity in many countries, and good environmental quality

is essential to attracting a significant slice of the tourism market, especially ecotourism. Ecotourism is defined as "traveling to relatively un-
disturbed or uncontaminated natural areas with the specific objective of
studying, admiring and enjoying the scenery and its wild plants and
animals, as well as any existing cultural manifestation" (Ceballos-Lascurain,
1988). In economic terms, ecotourism is a nonconsumptive use of
natural resources that increases their economic value. Developing regions that still have well-preserved natural areas can generally pursue
ecotourism as an alternative form of economic development (Alderman, 1994). This economic motivation can improve the political and
financial viability of environmental conservation initiatives.

Tourism has helped motivate environmental preservation in several developing countries. In Ecuador, the number of tourists steadily
grew during the 1970s and 1980s (Boo, 1990). Most of these tourists
came to enjoy Ecuador's cultural and natural attractions. Fifty-two percent
of tourists responding to an airport survey mentioned visiting protected
areas as the most important reason to come to Ecuador, especially
Galapagos National Park, a UNESCO World Heritage Site. Revenue
from entrance fees to Galapagos helped fund the creation and maintenance of other protected areas (Wallace, 1993). The Ecuadorian government, through the Ecuadorian Park Service, had worked on a new
national preservation strategy based on the creation of protected areas
since 1990 (Ceballos-Lascurain, 1996). However, Galapagos Park has
suffered from environmental degradation in the 2000s, as the number
of tourists and dwellers grew without control.

Costa Rica is another example of how nature-based tourism can
generate revenues and increase the economic and political viability of
environmental protection. Though some authors claim that legislation
is the most influential factor to promote environmental conservation
(Stem et al., 2003), ecotourism has played an important role as a driving
force to establish protected areas. More than 50 percent of Costa Rica's
tourists practiced ecotourism by visiting a protected area, according to
an airport survey (Boo, 1990). Tourism has become one of the nation's
most important economic activities. In 1993, tourism became the
country's top foreign exchange earner (Honey, 1999). In 1988, tourism
revenues totaled US$ 165 million, and constituted the third-largest
export activity (Chant, 1992, p. 91). Some critics argue that Costa
Rica's tourism is not much different from conventional tourism
(McLaren, 1998); since the 1980s Costa Rica has become an interna-
tionally recognized nature-based tourism destination and has some

characteristics of mass tourism (Chant, 1992; Weaver, 1999). Promoted initially by private tour operators, nature-based tourism was embraced by the national government as a high priority. Environmental protection became a buzzword, and environmentalism became part of the country's consciousness. Plans were promoted and laws were passed to give incentives to environmental protection and tourism promotion. At least 25 percent of Costa Rican territory is under some form of environmental protection in the end of the 1990s (Honey, 1999).

In this context, several public policy responses have been generated to promote environmental protection in regions with tourism development (Puppim de Oliveira, 2003). One of those responses is the creation of protected areas. It seems that tourism can create some of the positive conditions for spurring protected-area policies. In the last two decades, tourism has emerged as a driving force behind the establishment of protected areas in many developing countries. The need for environmental conservation as an asset in developing tourism activities is a powerful idea. Many governments have created protected areas as a result of pressures related to tourism development. They have been established to both promote nature-based tourism as well as control the environmental impacts of tourism development. Thus, tourism can be a driving force to the establishment of protected areas. The process of establishment of protected areas is connected with the role of the different actors in tourism development.

One of the main reasons for creating a large number of protected areas is to provide recreation for local populations and tourists (UNEP & WTO, 1992). The establishment of many protected areas is an attempt to attract tourists while protecting the environment from substantial change stemming from other activities as well as from tourism itself. Revenues from tourism can significantly contribute to maintenance of protected areas and encourage individuals and organizations to preserve the environment from which they profit.

Different kinds of tourism depend on different kinds of preservation and environments. Some protected areas are established to preserve fauna and flora, and visitors are generally allowed only in certain zones and kept at a certain distance from the animals. This is the case of some natural parks in Kenya. Other protected areas are established for game hunting, as are many game reserves in Africa. In these cases, the goal is to maintain animal populations at optimum levels for conservation and hunting. Still other areas are created primarily to preserve certain landscapes or geological formations, as in the case of Yellowstone. Finally, entire rural environments can also become protected areas. In England, several protected areas were established to preserve the cultural and natural environment of rural communities. Some of these areas contain more than 250,000 inhabitants (Nash, 1978). Many visitors come to enjoy this bucolic environment that was quickly disappearing.

Protected areas can provide recreation for a large number of people and generate considerable revenue. For example, the U.S. national park system is the largest tourist attraction in the world (Baker, 1990, quoted in UNEP & WTO, 1992); more than 270 million people visited these parks in 1989, and 266 millions in 2003 (NPS, 2003a). Visitors' spending impacts are significant, generating an estimated US$ 10.6 billion and providing 212,000 jobs in the neighboring communities in 2001 (NPS, 2003). State parks in the United States are even more popular, with over 500 million visitors in 2001. In Kenya, tourism in protected areas was the main source of foreign currency, bringing in US$ 400 million into the country in 1989 (UNEP & WTO, 1992). Part of the revenue from tourism was often reinvested into operating and maintaining protected areas. For many developing countries that lack financial resources, income from tourism is the only means and justification for protecting the environment by establishing protected areas.

Recently, other factors related to tourism have stimulated the establishment of protected areas. Governments have created protected areas to attract private and public investment in tourism. Protected areas guarantee private investors that disorderly development will not occur next to their projects. The Bahia State Tourism Secretariat has advertised and emphasized this aspect in its brochure for private investors (Bahia State Government, 1997). This also occurs when projects require financing from multilateral donors. In Bahia, the environmentally protected areas of Santo Antonio and Itacare were created as environmental safeguards to approve a project of road construction financed by multilateral organizations. Local governments have also established protected areas to attract investment from higher levels of government. Protected areas can signify that the local government is committed to controlling the impacts of tourism. Many municipalities in Bahia have tried to create protected areas to attract state tourism projects. Finally, protected areas have been advertised to attract tourists, particularly ecotourists. For instance, the municipality of Jandaira has published and distributed several brochures describing its main tourism attraction, the Mangue Seco APA (Prefeitura Municipal de Jandaira, n.d.).

However, even though tourism can attract funds for establishing and maintaining protected areas, it can also exert negative economic, environmental, and social impacts on protected areas (Buultjens et al., 2005). These impacts stem from construction of infrastructure, overuse of natural resources, and other activities that affect natural resources, fauna, flora, the landscape, and local culture. Thus, a balance must be struck between tourism and socioenvironmental conditions. Overcrowding or misuse of protected areas can pose a major threat to effective environmental management. Many protected areas have already suffered negative impacts. In Nepal, Annapurna and Sagarmatha national parks have been impacted heavily by tourism. The harvesting of wood for building and heating lodges, deterioration of vegetation by trekking, and the accumulation of large volumes of uncollected solid waste are some of the consequences of the growing tourism industry (Nepal, 2000). The number of tourists in Nepal, mostly trekkers, increased from under 10,000 in 1965 to over 240,000 in 1987 (Boo, 1990). Even some apparently low-impact activities such as birdwatching can have significant effects on the environment if they are not controlled. For example, large numbers of birdwatchers changed bird behavior in Loxahatchee National Wildlife Refuge in Florida (Burger & Gochfeld, 1998).

3.6 PROTECTED AREAS IN BRAZIL

3.6.1 Evolution of Environmental Institutions in the Brazilian State

During the 1970s,[3] Brazilian and international environmental groups started to protest Brazil's failure to respond to some of its environmental problems, such as the deforestation of the Amazon, the widespread industrial pollution in Cubatao (State of Sao Paulo), and the agreement between Brazil and Germany to build a series of nuclear reactors. After the United Nations Conference on the Human Environment in Stockholm in 1972, the Brazilian federal government decided to create the Special Secretariat for the Environment[4] in 1973. Many states, such as Sao Paulo and Rio de Janeiro, also decided to create their own environmental agencies. However, the staff of these national and state agencies was very limited in the beginning, and there was no comprehensive legislation or institutional structure to deal with most environmental problems (Loureiro & Pacheco, 1995).

In the 1980s, the legal and institutional structure for environmental policy and management was strengthened by the first comprehensive national environmental legislation: the National Environmental Policy in 1981. Also in the 1980s, the Ministry of Urban Development and the Environment was created (in 1985), and the National Environmental Council (Conama) was consolidated. Environmental NGOs participated with Conama when it was established in 1981, but their influence was limited while Brazil was under military dictatorship (until 1985), as political dissent during that period was uncommon and punishable. The democratization process after 1985 helped the increase in the environmental movements and NGOs, as well as the establishment of the Green Party (Partido Verde). In 1988, the environment received a special chapter in the new Brazilian constitution. At the state level, the 1980s were also crucial. States and municipalities generated their own environmental legislation, and environmental agencies and councils were established or enhanced.

The federal constitution of 1988 states that state and federal governments have the authority to legislate environmental matters.[5] The federal government establishes legislation stating general guidelines. Conama[6] specifies more detailed policy guidelines for implementing federal legislation. States create specific legislation according to their needs but must always follow federal guidelines.

Although the federal constitution does not mention that municipalities can also legislate on environmental matters, it does not stipulate the contrary. The federal constitution authorizes municipalities to enact legislation to achieve local interests, and these interests have been interpreted to include environmental resource protection (Puppim de Oliveira & Ogata, 1998).[7] However, environmental legislation at lower jurisdictional levels cannot contradict legislation passed at higher levels; in other words, municipal legislation cannot be less stringent than state legislation, and state legislation cannot be less stringent than federal legislation.

Regarding land-use rules, the federal constitution declares that municipalities should promote controlled land occupation through planning, land-use control, land subdivisions, and urban land development rules. The state and federal governments do not directly regulate land use, but they can intervene in land use rules when environmental protection is involved, such as in the case of environmentally protected areas in Bahia.

At the federal level in the 1980s, the ministry in charge of environmental affairs evolved into the Ministry of the Environment. Today, as states and municipalities have assumed responsibility for most aspects

of environment policy, federal activity involves establishing some additional national environmental legislation and implementation guidelines, and providing states with funds to pursue environmental policies
and projects. However, the federal government still exercises much control
over some renewable resources (such as fisheries and national forests),
licencing of offshore oil and nuclear activities, and administering federal
conservation units[8] through the newly created Chico Mendes Institute
linked to the Ministry of the Environment..

The institutional structure for establishing Brazilian environmental
policy is undergoing transition. Most of the states (including Bahia) hold
most of the responsibility for environmental protection. As some municipalities create additional institutional and legal capacity to cope with
certain environmental matters, states transfer responsibilities to them (for
example, responsibility for noise control has been transferred to some
municipalities, mainly the largest cities, as well as some licencing responsibilities of projects to local impacts). However, most of the small municipalities have little or no institutional or legal apparatus for environmental
protection. Some environmental responsibilities have also shifted to other
state agencies (e.g., some conservation units were under the State Agriculture Secretariat in Bahia in the beginning of the 1990s).

Because of all these institutional transitions, public accountability
for environmental protection can be often weak in Brazil (Ames &
Keck, 1997). Sometimes no public agency claims responsibility for certain
environmental problems (Puppim de Oliveira and Ogata, 1998). Other
times more than one public agency is involved in an environmental
matter, so responsibilities overlap. Although municipalities control land
use according to the federal constitution, many municipalities have no
institutional apparatus to implement land-use controls. In Bahia, out of
more than 400 municipalities, only Salvador had prepared a master plan
by 1996, even though federal law required master plans for municipalities over 20,000 inhabitants since 1988. Furthermore, federal and state
governments issue environmental legislation specifying land-use rules
that municipalities are supposed to follow, such as coastal management
plans. However, many municipalities have different land-use regulations
or lack the institutional apparatus to implement these upper-level regulations, so they rarely implement them.

3.6.2 Evolution of Protected Areas in Brazil

The 19-century U.S. concept of national parks motivated influential
personalities to suggest similar kinds of policies in Brazil (Padua, 1987).

In 1876, André Rebouças, a well-known engineer and public administrator, proposed creating two national parks: one surrounding the Sete
Quedas waterfall,[9] and another on the Bananal fluvial island.[10] Rebouças's
proposals did not receive much political support. However, the idea of
preserving natural resources through protected areas resurfaced in the
mid-1930s with debates over the first forest code. This code, approved
in 1934, defined three kinds of protected areas: national parks, national
forests, and protected forests.[11]

In 1937, the first national park was created: the Itatiaia National
Park, a forested mountain chain used as a vacation refuge for many
well-to-do citizens from Sao Paulo and Rio de Janeiro, then the Brazilian capital. The objective underlying the creation of these parks was
preservation of unique natural areas with scenic and scientific value
(WWF, 1994, quoting the Brazilian constitution of 1937).

The federal government created several more protected areas until
the establishment of a new forest code in 1965. This code divided protected areas into two groups. No resources could be exploited in the first
group (National Parks and Biological Reserve[12]). In the second group,
protected areas would be used for economic or social objectives (national
forests). The forest code also defined areas under *permanent preservation*,
which included several categories of ecosystems such as land abutting
water bodies and steep terrain (Governo do Estado da Bahia, 1998).

The next significant legislative change occurred in 1981, when a
law established two other kinds of protected areas: ecological stations[13]
and environmentally protected areas (APAs). From that point on, dis-
tinctions among so many kinds of protected areas began to blur, as
presidential decrees created four other categories of protected areas
from 1984 to 1990: ecological reserves, areas of relevant ecological
interest, extractivist reserves, and private reserves. However, the number
of protected areas grew significantly, to 142 by 1991, and to 1,281 by
2003 or 18.5 percent of the terrestrial area (UNEP, 2004).

The new categories were created mostly by bureaucrats in the
Brazilian Institute of Forest Development (IBDF), an obscure federal
agency. Sometimes these officials created a new kind of protected area
to account for the characteristics of a type of region not yet covered.
Rivalries among different federal bureaucracies also stimulated the creation of new categories. For example, an ecological station was not very
different from a biological or ecological reserve. However, the former
category was created because officials in the Federal Secretariat for the
Environment (SEMA) wanted to establish their own protected areas

without interference from the other federal environmental bureaucracy, the Brazilian Institute of Forest Development (IBDF), which SEMA considered to be representing pro-timber interests. By establishing a new category, SEMA could prevent over 3.2 million hectares of primary forests from falling into the hands of timber companies (Nogueira Neto, 1992).

The federal constitution of 1988 suggests that "public institutions" can set aside conservation areas. All three levels of government (federal, state, and municipal) can designate parts of their territories as "conservation units." In 1987, Conama made an attempt to streamline the classification system of protected areas by defining ten categories.[14] Conama and government agencies discussed these categories before submitting the National System of Conservation Units (SNUC) for approval by the National Congress in 1992. Debates over these formal categories for protected areas (or what SNUC calls conservation units) lasted several years. SNUC was approved in July, 2000 (Ministério do Meio Ambiente, 2004). According to this new system, there are two kinds of protected areas: areas for integral protection and areas for sustainable use. Areas for integral protection include the following categories: biological reserves, ecological stations, natural monuments, wildlife refuges, and parks. Areas for sustainable use include: area of relevant ecological interest, fauna reserves, environmentally protected areas (APAs), extractive reserves, reserves for sustainable development, private reserves of the natural heritage (RPPN), and public forests. Those areas can be created at the federal, state, or municipal level.

These categories accomplish different objectives, and each has its own rules regarding land use, property rights, administration, and environmental management structure. For example, in some conservation units, such as national and state parks, almost no development is allowed, and private land should be expropriated and landowners compensated. In other categories, such as APAs, expropriation is not necessary and certain kinds of development are allowed. Because of their flexibility regarding land use and property rights, APAs have become one of the most popular conservation units (Corte, 1995).

As mentioned in a previous section, the establishment and implementation of protected areas present several obstacles at the government level, such as political obstruction, lack of funding, insufficient institutional capacity, and resistance at the local level. These obstacles are especially difficult to overcome in developing countries, like Brazil, where environmental protection is not often a top priority. Because most of the responsibility for establishing protected areas rests with governments, the effectiveness and efficiency of any protected-area policy depend on the importance governments assign to protected areas and on their ability to create and maintain them. Social, environmental, and political conditions greatly influence the outcome of protected-area policies. Moreover, the way governments devise their organizational structure to implement and oversee protected areas seems fundamental to shaping the results. In the last two decades, tourism development has influenced the establishment of protected areas.

The next chapter covers the case of environmentally protected areas in the state of Bahia, Brazil. The state government's determination to promote tourism as a priority of the economic development agenda was fundamental in explaining the creation and implementation of many protected areas, especially in zones with tourism potential. Several state agencies that worked in tourism and infrastructure development became involved with protected areas. Thus, the association of protected areas with the potential benefits of tourism, and the organizational arrangement for dealing with protected areas, are crucial to understanding why many of the political, institutional, and financial obstacles to establishing protected areas were overcome in Bahia.

4
_____

Overcoming the Obstacles for Policy Implementation

The Case of the Establishment of Protected Areas in Bahia

4.1 INTRODUCTION

T he two roles of governments—promoter of economic develop ment and protector of environmental quality—may seem in conflict, and they are in many cases. Especially in developing countries, economic interests tend to have a priority in the government's development agenda. This creates obstacles to the implementation of environmental policies. However, the bias against environmental policies can be reversed by introducing concerns over environmental protection into the mainstream development agenda by decentralizing environmental policy implementation to development-oriented agencies under certain conditions. Empirical evidence of the results of decentralization of environmental policies to development-oriented organizations is given in this chapter for the protected areas of the Brazilian state of Bahia.[1] In Bahia, the decentralization and administration of protected areas among several agencies at the state level primarily accounted for the ability of the state to establish a large number of protected areas. Horizontal decentralization explains how the state was able to overcome the political, financial, and institutional obstacles to environmental policy implementation.

The chapter is divided into four parts. First, it covers the background of the state of Bahia and its environmental management policies, especially its policies toward environmentally protected areas. Second, the chapter analyzes the case at the state level and how the decentralization of protected area policy to development-oriented agencies is fundamental in explaining the creation of a large number of protected areas. Third, it examines the participation of local actors in the implementation of state policies.

4.2 THE BACKGROUND OF BAHIA AND TOURISM DEVELOPMENT

Brazil's Northeast region, where Bahia is located, comprises nine states and has a population of over 47.8 million inhabitants in an area of over 1.5 million km^2 (28.3 percent of Brazilian territory). This population alone is greater than that of any other South American country, while the surface area of the Northeast is second only to Argentina. Within this region, the state of Bahia has both the largest economy (GDP of R\$ 48.2 billion in 2000, or approximately US\$ 20 billion) and population (13 million in 2000) (IBGE, 2005).

The economic and social indicators of the Northeast have, however, lagged behind the rest of Brazil for many decades. For example, in comparison with the national average, the Northeastern income per capita is less than half and its illiteracy rate is more than double. The state of Bahia is slightly better off with a per capita income of 57 percent of the Brazilian average. In terms of income inequalities, its Gini coefficient is higher than that of Brazil as a whole, which is one of the highest in the world.

For many decades, the Northeast has been a symbol of backwardness for many Brazilians and a challenge for regional policy makers to reduce the disparities between the Northeast and the most developed regions in southern Brazil. Since the 1950s, several regional policies have aimed at attracting national or international private investment through fiscal incentives and facilitation of financing. Two major public regional development institutions managed these policies, both managed by the federal government: the Bank of the Northeast and the Superintendency for the Development of the Northeast (SUDENE).[2] In the last decades, the Northeast has indeed attracted important investments in chemicals, pulp and paper, and textiles. However, these investments have been insufficient to foster sustained development and break the country's south–north disparities.

Since the 1990s, tourism has been the focus of regional policymakers and the hope for economic development. The main tourist attractions in the Northeast are its costal ecosystems and cultural attractions. The region possesses a significant potential for the development of tourism: warm climate year-round, cultural diversity, and over 2,500 km of attractive seashore, especially in Bahia, which has the longest seashore in Brazil with more than 1,100 km. The region's white sand beaches make idyllic tropical settings of clear ocean water, spotted by dunes, lagoons, mangroves, and typical villages framed by coconut trees. In this context, tourism has increasingly become a key economic activity and a good prospect for the continuing economic growth of Bahia.

4.2.1 State Tourism Development Program

The Bahian state tourism development program defined a series of infrastructure projects designed to attract private investment (Bahia State Government, 1997). A landmark was the establishment of Prodetur-NE in 1991, the regional tourism development program for the Brazilian Northeast (Ministry of Economy, Treasury, and Planning; Bank of the Northeast, & Inter-American Development Bank, 1992). Prodetur-NE consisted of a series of projects with financing from the Bank of the Northeast, based on loans from the Inter-American Development Bank (IDB) matched by funds from the state governments. Under Prodetur, the public sector invested over US$ 600 million in tourism infrastructure and services in the Northeast by the year 2002 (Table 4.1). In the second phase, there were plans to invest around US$ 800 million, totalling US$ 1.4 billion (Banco do Nordeste 2005). The Bank of the Northeast coordinated the program, but state governments were responsible for drawing up their own tourism plans. These plans would identify priority projects, which would be evaluated and approved by the Bank of the Northeast under the supervision of the IDB. Under this program, the Bank of the Northeast–approved tourism infrastructure projects in Bahia cost about US$ 337 million (Table 4.2).

Besides Prodetur-NE, the state of Bahia planned more public investments in areas with tourism potential. These investments would total US$ 2.55 billion in the period from 1995 to 2002 (Bahia State Government, 2005). State officials also expected to attract more than US$ 5 billion in private investment between 1995 and 2012 (Bahia State Government, 1997, 2005). All these investments impacted somehow Bahia's environmental policies.

Table 4.1 The first phase of tourism investments in the Brazilian Northeast and Bahia within Prodetur-NE

Kind of Project	Prodetur-NE in the Northeast (in millions of US$)	Bahia (in millions of US$)
Airports	222.7	104.4
Roads (transportation)	139.5	47.0
Sanitation	142.9	46.3
Restoration of historical buildings	45.6	9.0
Studies and evaluations	10.5	3.2
Institutional development	20.2	2.3
Total	**601.5**	**213.4**

Source: Banco do Nordeste, 2005.

As tourism became a priority for economic development, the governors of Bahia, and the Northeast in general, gave a lot of political importance to the position of State Secretariat of Culture and Tourism (Sectur), as well as a lot of financial resources to policy implementation with funds that came also from the federal government and multilateral organizations like the Inter-American Development Bank (IDB). Secretariats of tourism have had significant resources and power since 1990s and even got involved and developed institutional capacity to deal with environmental policies, as those are fundamental to get their projects approved timely by outside sources of funding.

Table 4.2 Planned tourism investments in Bahia, 1991–2002

Kind of Project	Amount (US$ 1,000)
Ports and airports	12,640
Roads	177,308
Sanitation	56,980
Energy	15,771
Restoration of historical buildings	9.471
Equipment and services	46,928
Studies and evaluations	10,000
Marketing	5,000
Human resource development	3,000
Total	**337,100**

Source: Banco do Nordeste, 1997.

4.3 UNDERSTANDING ENVIRONMENTAL POLICY AND APAS IN BRAZIL AND BAHIA

Over the last 30 years, the landscape of the Brazilian State of Bahia underwent rapid transformation, especially along the coast. Huge industrial clusters such as Camaçari and Aratu grew up. Agricultural activities also expanded along the coastal strip. Logging advanced toward the few remaining areas of the Atlantic Forest, especially in the southern part of the state. Coastal cities have grown exponentially without much urban planning. Tourism has spread rapidly around several towns, such as Porto Seguro and Ilheus. After infrastructure improvements, the frontier for tourism development advanced to the northern coast.

Many of these activities took place without proper environmental planning, causing problems such as air and water pollution, deforestation, and destruction of officially protected ecosystems,[3] such as the Atlantic Forest in southern Bahia. This forest was thought to have some of the world's highest tree biodiversity (Conservation International, 1995).[4] Because the southern part of the state had one of the fastest-growing tourism and forestry industries in Brazil, the Atlantic Forest quickly disappeared over the last few decades (Figure 4.1; cf. SEI, 1995). Moreover, many traditional communities—which house some of the poorest and most powerless people in the region—were transformed both physically and culturally.

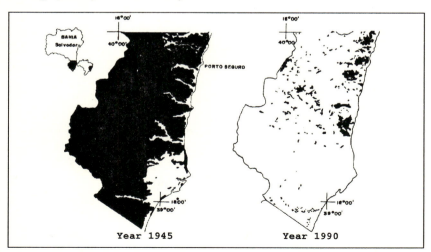

Figure 4.1 Change in the Atlantic Forest in Southern Bahia between 1945 and 1990. (The area in black was Atlantic Forest.) *Source:* Analise & Dados, 1994, p. 108.

At the outset, unrestrained development along the coast was not viewed as a problem since it was occurring in isolated areas. More recently, however, the tourism model of development spread to larger areas, and tourism gained support as an attractive regional economic development stimulus. Governmental agencies and some parts of civil society in Bahia realized that weak environmental management was a potential threat to the long-term viability of tourism along Bahia's rich coast,[5] as well as to other areas with tourism potential. If uncontrolled development continued, the natural environment and traditional coastal communities would be seriously affected, and consequently, the potential for tourism could be undermined in the future.

Since the nation's democratization in 1985, actors in civil society, such as nongovernmental organizations (NGOs) and community organizations, have increasingly pressured governmental authorities to take greater responsibility for protecting environmental resources and the well-being of coastal communities. After the military dictatorship ended in 1985, the number of NGOs in Brazil grew significantly (Bernardes & Nanne, 1994), especially environmental NGOs (Viola, 1992). Following this pattern, the number of environmental NGOs in the state of Bahia increased impressively in the last decades (Figure 4.2), particularly when compared with other states in the Northeast (Table 4.3). Between 1985 and 1992, the number of NGOs grew from 5 to 40. By 2000, it was estimated that more than 200 environmental NGOs existed in Bahia (CRA, 2004).

Many of these groups were created with specific objectives, such as defending a certain ecosystem or protesting against an environmental problem or disaster. For example, the NGO Pro-Tamar Foundation was created to protect marine turtles, which were threatened almost to extinction by rapid development of the seashore.[6] The Movement for the Defense of Sao Francisco River (MDSF) was established to mobilize the local population regarding environmental problems in the river basin, such as pollution and sedimentation. Most of these NGOs acted regionally or locally. Only a few had links to NGOs in other states or countries.[7] However, NGOs in Bahia were important in environmental decision making. Some of them (e.g., Gamba, Germen, and Ascae) regularly denounced environmental degradation and actively participated in the decisions of the state environmental council (CEPRAM).

In several cases, NGOs have acted in defense of the environment and powerless local communities. For example, in the coastal village of

Balbino in the state of Ceara, developers burned houses and threatened villagers with death to force them off their land, which was partially covered by mangroves. With the support of NGOs, communities highlighted these issues in the mainstream media and pressured local and state authorities to take action to protect local people and award them title to the land. In the end, the state government of Ceara legalized local land titles and created an environmentally protected area (APA) in the region to avoid land speculation. In Bahia, local inhabitants in the Abaete APA denounced a construction project that violates APA guidelines and tried to stop it in court, even though developers had a municipal construction permit (*A Tarde*, 1997a, 1997b, 1998; Ministério Público Federal, 1997).

In Bahia, policy guidelines to implement state legislation were specified by the State Environmental Council (CEPRAM).[8] CEPRAM has functioned since 1972 and is the first state environmental council created in Brazil. It is in charge of the main decisions concerning environmental policy at the state level and gives the final word about some environmental licencing processes. One third of its members are from governmental agencies, one third are representatives of entrepreneurs and

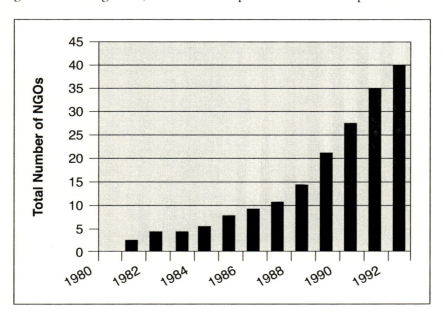

Figure 4.2 Total number of environmental NGOs in Bahia over time.
Source: Mater Natura—Instituto de Estudos Ambientais, 1996.

Table 4.3 Number of environmental NGOs in the states of the Brazilian Northeast

State	Number of NGOs per one million inhabitants (1995)
Bahia	3.9
R. G. Norte	2.9
Pernambuco	1.7
Paraiba	1.3
Alagoas	1.2
Maranhao	1.0
Ceara	0.9
Sergipe	0

Source: Mater Natura—Instituto de Estudos Ambientais (1996), Almanaque Abril (1995).

workers, and one third are representatives of environmental NGOs. Certain kinds of development projects over a certain size had to be approved by CEPRAM to gain a state development permit. CEPRAM members convene once a month to screen important development projects and to discuss the introduction of environmental policies based on state laws and decrees. In the 1990s it was modernized, with the public given access to its processes, so CEPRAM analyzed an increasing number of projects and polices (see Figure 4.3 for the number of projects analyzed by CEPRAM). The public agency in charge of implementing environmental policies used to be the Center for Environmental Resources (CRA), which was under the State Secretariat of Planning, Science, and Technology (SEPLANTEC, or Secretaria de Planejamento, Ciência e Tecnologia) until the year 2000, when it became part of a newly created Secretariat of the Environment and Water Resources.

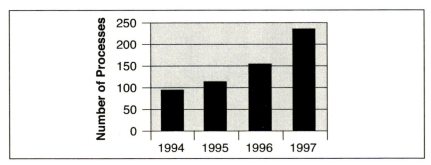

Figure 4.3 Number of processes analyzed by CEPRAM over time. *Sources:* Centro de Recursos Ambientais, n.d.; CEPRAM, 1999.

Since the beginning of the1990s, another group of public actors expanded its role in environmental protection: public prosecutors (similar to U.S. district attorneys). According to the constitution, public prosecutors "should promote inquiries and public processes in order to protect the environment and other public or collective interests."[9] In Bahia, the state court system created a department of public prosecutors specializing in environmental law in the 1990s. These prosecutors have initiated several cases against individuals, companies, and state and municipal agencies, sometimes contesting development permits and environmental management in APAs. For example, in a case brought by public prosecutors in Bahia, the construction company MRM started a development project in the Abaete APA in Salvador with authorization from the municipal government. However, this project broke several APA land-use rules. The municipality had granted permission for the project without consulting state authorities. As a result, public prosecutors sued MRM and the municipal government (A. Tarde, 1997; and Ministério Público Federal, 1997). Public prosecutors, thus, have become one of the catalyzers of enforcement of environmental laws, even becoming the overseers of public agencies in charge of environmental protection at the federal, state, and municipal levels.

The mere identification of a problem is rarely sufficient to spur determined state action. There had been several obstacles to an expanded state government role in environmental protection, especially the creation of conservation units. First, zoning and other land-use controls were interpreted in the Brazilian constitution as municipal responsibilities. Therefore, the state had limited power to intervene in these issues. Second, traditional approaches to protecting sensitive environmental areas usually involved the expropriation of land. This would be extremely costly for the entire area involved in Bahia and probably well beyond the resources the state had available for environmental protection.

Third, in the past, the few preserved areas in the state were mostly national parks under the jurisdiction of IBAMA,[10] a federal institution, over which the state had very little influence. IBAMA has suffered from serious institutional problems, such as the lack of funding and personnel since the 1990s. Thus, a sharp increase in the area and number of federally protected areas was unlikely. Fourth, the state environmental agency (CRA) alone could not do much to carry out a widespread policy of creating protected areas because it lacked the funds, the technical and institutional capacity, and the political capital. Therefore, a new approach was necessary to bring the state into the process of protecting the environment in areas with tourism potential. As we will see, the creation of APAs and the involvement of various agencies proved to be an alternative in overcoming some of the problems mentioned above.

4.4 EVOLUTION OF ENVIRONMENTAL MANAGEMENT IN BAHIA AND THE OUTCOME: THE CREATION OF APAS

The growth of tourism and the elaboration of the state tourism plan in the beginning of the 1990s influenced the environmental policies in Bahia. Before the 1990s, the number and area of conservation units in Bahia were extremely modest. Only two environmentally protected areas (APAs) and a few ecological stations and parks existed (CRA, 2004). These conservation units were administrated by various institutions, such as the federal environmental agency (IBAMA), municipalities, and diverse state agencies (agriculture, education, and culture secretariats). Few of those protected areas had even a minimal management structure or plan.[11]

At that time, the state environmental agency (CRA)[12] had little involvement with protected areas. CRA was created in 1983 mostly to control industrial pollution, especially from the huge Camaçari petrochemical complex,[13] which started operating in the late 1970s. CRA thus had limited organizational capacity. Although development in Bahia had expanded into fragile ecosystems, the state had done little to take a more active role in land-use planning or protecting ecosystems. Environmental problems related to ecosystem degradation, such as deforestation and illegal fishing, were generally addressed by the state branch of IBAMA or very casually by CRA. Moreover, once CRA was still under the Secretariat of Planning, Science, and Technology (SEPLANTEC), it had limited political autonomy and power and thus was not in a position to politically promote environmental protection. Therefore, before 1990, policies for preserving ecosystems were not a priority for institutions at the state level, and there was little political momentum for an expansion of the state's role in this area.

However, tourism changed this institutional environment (May & Pastuk, 1996). Tourism had expanded considerably in Bahia in the 1980s, especially in the coastal regions outside Salvador (Table 4.4).

Table 4.4 Hosting capacity in the different coastal zones in Bahia in 1980 and 1993

Region	Number of Beds in 1980	Number of Beds in 1993	Annual Growth Rate (%)
Salvador Metropolitan Region	9,600	15,170	4.46
Northern Coast	800	5,760	47.69
Southern Coast	3,300	29,929	62.07

Source: Bahia State Government (1997)

Moreover, state planners saw great potential for nature-based tourism on some of unexplored parts of the Bahian coast. Because the state decided to invest heavily in tourism infrastructure to organize and spur further growth in that sector, many worried that tourism could harm fragile ecosystems over large areas without appropriate environmental protection measures.

Some NGOs represented on the state environmental council (CEPRAM) started to question some aspects of those development projects, especially the construction of roads that would provide access to pristine environments. State officials had to respond somehow to these demands. Therefore, APAs were the result of discussions in meetings among influential state officials from different state secretariats about how to control the environmental impacts of this planned growth in tourism. These officials proposed to create APAs where development projects were planned or tourism development was occurring.

In the past decade the state of Bahia started to aggressively implement a policy of creating APAs in regions with potential for tourism development. The number of APAs and the area covered by them grew significantly (Figures 4.4 and 4.5)—from two in 1990 to more than 28 effectively created by 2004. The area covered by APAs expanded over 200 times, from 13,700 hectares in 1990 to more than 3 million hectares in 2004 (CRA, 2004).

In ideal terms, the creation of a state APA would transfer certain development rights in the region from private landowners and municipal governments[14] to a management council under a plan coordinated by one or more state agencies.[15] APAs permit broader involvement of

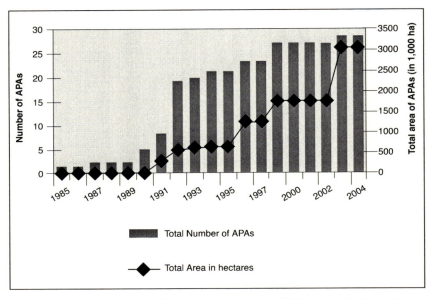

Figure 4.4 Environmentally protected areas (APAs) in Bahia. *Source:* CRA, 2004.

the state government, local community groups, and civil society in land-use regulations, usually controlled by municipal governments. Moreover, contrary to the situation in areas of strict preservation, such as state or national parks, no land expropriation is necessary to create an APA, thereby reducing the costs associated with buying land as well as possible conflicts with private landowners.

Two main objectives led the government of Bahia to create APAs. The first was to preserve important, fragile ecosystems in regions undergoing rapid development, especially tourism development on the coast. In general, APAs created for this reason have very restrictive zoning rules, allowing only low-impact development.

The second objective was to use APAs to mitigate environmental impacts of large development projects such as roads. Many of these projects were part of the state tourism development plan. These APAs are usually large, sometimes encompassing more than 100,000 hectares, and their zoning system is less restrictive. These areas sometimes include semi-urbanized areas and territories in several municipalities (e.g., the North Coast and Santo Antonio APAs).

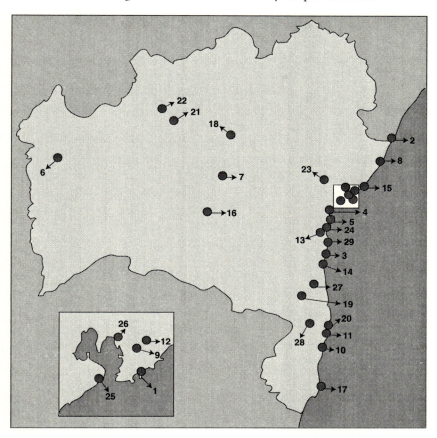

1. Lagos e Dunas do Abaete
2. Mangue Seco
3. Costa de Itacare/Serra Grande
4. Guaibim
5. Ilhas Tinhare/Boipeba
6. Bacia do Rio de Janeiro
7. Marimbus/Iraquara
8. Litoral Norte (Northern Coast)
9. Bacia Hidrográfica Joanes
10. Caraíva/Trancoso
11. Coroa Vermelha
12. Rio Capivara
13. Cachoeira de Pancada Grande
14. Lagoa Encantada
15. Lagoa de Guarajuba
16. Serra do Barbado
17. Ponta da Baleia/Abrolhos
18. Gruta dos Brejoes/Veredas
   do Romao Gramacho
19. Vale das Cascatas
20. Santo Antonio
21. Lagoa de Itaparica
22. Dunas e Veredas do Baixo
   Medio Sao Francisco
23. Lago de Pedra do Cavalo
24. Pratigi
25. Recife das Pinaunas
26. Lagoa CCC
27. Serra das Candeias
28. Itapebi
29. Peninsula de Marau

Figure 4.5—Names and locations of APAs in Bahia (29 were planned, but until 2004 only 28 were effectively created). *Source:* CRA, 2004.

The management of APAs was under the control of several state agencies and municipal governments. At the state level, the agencies in charge of coordinating the process of creating, planning, and managing APAs until 1999 were the Bahia Tourism Authority (Bahiatursa),[16] under SECTUR, and the State Environmental Agency (CRA) and Company for the Development of the Metropolitan Region (CONDER),[17] both under SEPLANTEC at that time.

The process of establishing APAs followed two procedural levels. The first level concerned the policy process at the state level (central level). Here, the process usually had several stages, as follows. Initially a state governmental organization proposed an APA to the state governor. After an APA was designated by the state legislation, state agencies (with the involvement of local governments and populations) coordinated the preparation of a management plan subjected to approval by the State Environmental Council (CEPRAM). Finally, state agencies prepared themselves to enforce the APA guidelines stipulated in the plan by building their own institutional capacity. The second procedural level involved implementation at the local level in which state agencies and local actors worked together to support the enforcement of APA guidelines. State agencies needed the participation of local actors to improve their enforcement capacity. The focus of this book is on the first level of state implementation.

Decentralization aided the process of protected area creation for several reasons. First, because development agencies were involved in APAs, they gained political support at the state level. These agencies, now involved in protected-area policy, had a political interest in creating APAs instead of blocking them. Second, financing for APAs grew because well-funded agencies were creating APAs, and they also attracted alternative sources of funding. Third, competition among several state agencies in administering APAs prompted them to improve their institutional capacity by hiring new people, investing in training, and buying equipment. The three state agencies involved in APAs also tried to improve their institutional capacity to show that they could handle and lead this new environmental task. Finally, local actors were less likely to oppose APAs because they associated APAs with development agencies and projects for their areas, not with land-use restrictions by the state. In the sections below, each of these four reasons are analyzes in more detail.

4.5 ESTABLISHMENT OF PROTECTED AREAS IN BAHIA: OBTAINING POLITICAL, INSTITUTIONAL, AND FINANCIAL SUPPORT

In this section I argue that the fact that APA policymaking and implementation involved various decentralized state agencies (horizontal decentralization), instead of being concentrated in the state environmental agency (CRA), is the primary reason why large number of APAs were established. I explain how this arrangement overcame the four obstacles to the establishment of protected areas described in chapter 3: the lack of political support, financial resources, institutional capacity, and cooperation at the local level.

4.5.1 Getting Political Support at the State Level from Pro-Development Actors

In developing countries, one main obstacle to the implementation of environmental policies is the lack of political support. Environmental policies tend to get little political support because many politicians, policymakers, and civil society in general associate environmental protection with restrictions in other spheres of development, particularly economic development. Sometimes, there are a lot of discourses on sustainable development and environmental protection, but not much is implemented as economic development becomes the priority. In order to be prioritized, environmental protection needs to be linked with economic initiatives, such as tourism development. One way to do that is to transfer certain responsibilities of environmental policy implementation to development-oriented agencies. This could bring political support from development-oriented agencies to the environmental agenda, as they would be directly interested in environmental policy implementation. In the case of APAs in Bahia, two development-oriented agencies, Sectur and Conder, had the responsibility of APA implementation, which led to a growing interest and political support at the state level because the APAs were linked to tourism development.

Creating conservation units (protected areas) requires enough political clout to prompt the state governor[18] to deliver a decree. Before the 1990s, the state governor had little interest in creating large conservation units. Traditional conservation units required the state to expropriate land, which could provoke both financial and political problems; expropriation consumes large amounts of resources, and the state must confront local politicians and powerful Brazilian agricultural interests. Moreover, elected leaders, state public officials, and civil society did not push the governor in this direction. Besides, the agency that would be naturally in charge of conservation units (CRA) had little technical expertise or political influence to propose a broad conservation policy. Development agencies, meanwhile, had no interest in conservation units before the 1990s.[19] In this institutional environment, few conservation units of significant size were created at the state level before 1990,[20] and no state agency had the specialized staff to pursue a comprehensive protected-area policy.

The proposal to decentralize responsibility for creating and administering APAs provoked competition among different state agencies. Although the state environmental agency had a mandate to deal with environmental matters, it was not the only agency interested in APAs, as APAs do allow some kinds of development, such as industrial districts or dense urban sites. APAs can be viewed as the environmental part of a development project, in the way that the Northern Coast APA was the environmental mitigation measure legitimizing construction of a long road crossing the region, the Green Line Road. Thus other state agencies had good reason to jump into the APA "business" as part of a tourism-related environmental strategy or urban development plans.

Involvement with APA administration gave government agencies considerable leverage for requesting resources. Agencies can request state funds to implement APAs (Table 4.5) or attract funding from national and international organizations, as in the agreement between Conder and the English ODA for the Northern Coast APA. Agencies inexperienced in environmental matters found they could extend their project "portfolios" if they developed the institutional capacity to perform the job, thereby gaining power and political influence. For instance, Conder had acquired considerable environmental expertise since its commitment to the Northern Coast APA. It even assisted the state environmental agency (CRA) in elaborating the management plan for the Tinhare-Boipeba APA.

Finally, by expanding into the environmental arena, development agencies could satisfy most of the environmental requirements for their own development projects, limiting interference by the environmental agency in their jobs. Sectur had significantly engaged in environmental management since the beginning of the implementation of its state tourism development plan, needing CRA only to approve its plans.

Any important environmental decision in Bahia—whether environmental policies or development projects with potentially negative environmental impacts—must pass through the State Environmental Council (CEPRAM). Because representatives of environmental NGOs constituted one third of CEPRAM, any project in Bahia with significant environmental consequences very likely needed their political support. These organizations had played an important role in environmental decision making since the 1980s. The other two thirds of CEPRAM members were divided evenly between representatives of state agencies and both employers' and employees' unions.

Development actors and environmental forces needed each other to approve their interests in CEPRAM. On the one hand, development agencies and developers' unions had their seats in CEPRAM, but they did not have the majority of the members. Thus they had to convince some other members to approve their development projects, including environmental NGOs and the state environmental agency.[21] On the other hand, environmental organizations and agencies had to get the support of many development actors to introduce or change any environmental policy or project. As a result, the environmental agency (CRA), without political support from development actors, would likely fail to introduce wide environmental measures that could restrain development or are too expensive to implement, such as the creation of conservation units. However, development agencies were more likely to succeed in approving wider environmental policies because they would probably get the political support of environmental groups and agencies, and were less likely to be blocked by development actors. Members of CEPRAM were supportive of the establishment of several APAs in the state. The environmentally friendly members saw APAs as ensuring some legal and policy structures to curb environmental degradation in the areas of rapid tourism growth. Development members regarded APAs as a tool for attracting future investors, as well as environmental safeguards of their development projects in order to have them approved by CEPRAM.

Development-oriented agencies, such as State Secretariat of Culture and Tourism (Sectur) and the Company for the Development of the Metropolitan region (CONDER), had their own reasons for supporting the creation of APAs, but under their own control. First, if APA administration was assigned to some other agency (CRA, for example) that agency could complicate approval of later development projects within the APA. Having an APA under its own control would allow a development-oriented agency to be more flexible in pursuing its development interests. In a few cases this had already happened. For example, in the Santo Antonio APA, the initial zoning code was changed to accommodate the interests of tourism investors. Municipal officials, developers, and local civil society stakeholders negotiated the change with state authorities before approving the final zoning code, as in the case of Santa Cruz Cabralia municipality.

Nonenvironmental agencies also wanted to control APAs because no other agency had experience in managing them, and it did not want to delay implementation and thus lose financing opportunities. At that time the state environmental agency (CRA) had no institutional capacity to manage protected areas, so it would be unlikely to finish the job in a timely manner. For example, Sectur also presented itself as an environmentally friendly agency when selling Bahia to tourism investors; several Sectur brochures highlight ecotourism and its relation to APAs.[22] Sectur's involvement in environmental management would help promote itself as an environmentally friendly agency. Finally, environmental projects could attract more state resources for implementing projects like APAs. Handing these projects to other agencies would mean foregoing opportunities to create in-house jobs.

Other development agencies involved in the state tourism program, including the Secretariat of Industry and Commerce and the Secretariat of Transportation, also lent political support to the new protected areas. These agencies were responsible for constructing roads and other projects and hence were eager to gain environmental safeguards for them. The Secretariat of Planning was also involved through Conder, which is a subsidiary agency. The interest of development agencies prompted state legislators to approve the APAs with little opposition.

CRA acted as an observer in this process, monitoring the activities of the other agencies and working on two relatively small APAs (Mangue Seco and Guaibim APAs). Although CRA was not in charge of creating all the APAs, it took advantage of the environmental momentum in the mid-1990s to submit applications to the governor for approval for areas such as APAs in Bacia do Rio de Janeiro, Lagoa de Itaparica, Dunas e Veredas do Baixo Medio Sao Francisco, and Lago de Pedra do Cavalo. Furthermore, CRA's role would increase when the APAs' management plans were elaborated, since CRA was by law the only agency that has the power to impose environmental sanctions.[23] In fact, the state government granted the responsibility for administering all APAs to CRA in 1999. Thus, the involvement of development-oriented organizations at the state level (Conder and Sectur) was fundamental to get political support for the establishment of APAs in the various levels, but once they were established, CRA started to manage them.

Therefore, the involvement of development agencies (Conder and Sectur) in the implementation of an environmental policy (creation of APAs) was key in giving political clout to environmental interests. This increased the support for the implementation of APAs in Bahia because those agencies were politically important and enjoyed broad political support for the environmental agenda.

4.5.2 Funding APAs by Involving Nonenvironmental Agencies

The involvement of development-oriented agencies in environmental policy can increase the amount of financial resources available for policy implementation in developing countries. In general, those agencies have larger budgets and can bring resources from different sources to environmental projects, if they are linked to their own development policies. The amount of resources from nonenvironmental agencies can be much larger than those available for environmental agencies. It is possible that a small percentage of resources deviated to environmental policies from a development project is larger than the budget of the environmental agency. For example, the environmental component of a tourism development program can be significantly larger than what this component would be if implemented separately.

In Bahia, the involvement of nonenvironmental agencies in APA policy also helped to attract extra funding for the protected areas. State decrees had created only two APAs by the early 1990s, Abaete and Gruta dos Brejoes APAs, which were intended to protect environmentally important regions under development pressure without expropriating private property. However, no attempt had been made to develop management plans or enforce environmental guidelines. Governmental organizations lacked much of the necessary technical expertise, and the environmental agency had no financial resources to hire outside consultants.

Because the Green Line Road was a priority of the state government, and the Northern Coast APA was needed to appease investors, lenders, and members of CEPRAM, Conder could raise funds for implementing it. By 1997 Conder had invested more than US$ 2.2 million in managing the Northern Coast APA. That amount was less than 20 percent of Conder's budget for projects[24] but more than 40 percent of CRA's total 1997 budget.

In 1990 the State Secretariat of Culture and Tourism (Sectur) also undertook a series of studies to define projects in the state tourism development plan within the Tourism Development Program (Prodetur). The plan included an analysis of the potential environmental impacts of each "touristic zone," as well as mitigation procedures to satisfy the demands of the lending organizations and CEPRAM. State officials wanted to attract private investors interested in low-density and upscale coastal resorts, who did not want unplanned development nearby. Municipal governments, however, often did not have the institutional capacity to impose land-use rules, even though the constitution assigns them responsibility for such rules. The solution was the creation of state APAs in areas with tourism potential.

As a result of the tourism development plan, Sectur proposed the creation of eight APAs, all approved by decree between 1993 and 1994. Sectur's accomplishments in elaborating the management plans for these APAs were remarkable (Table 4.6). Between 1995 and 1999, the agency generated seven plans—more than the sum of those elaborated by all other agencies by March, 1999. Sectur's APAs contained over 388,000 hectares—more than 66 percent of the total APA area with management plans. Sectur's efficiency in developing management plans stemmed from the resources it gathered for environmental management while implementing the state tourism plan. In total, Sectur invested over US$ 14 million in APA management, not counting personnel costs (see Table 4.5)—that is, $2^1/_2$ times CRA's total budget of US$ 5.7 million in 1997.

Sectur could raise funds for these management plans through annual budget requests and through Prodetur, the state tourism plan (Banco do Nordeste, 1996a). APAs were the state's guarantee to lenders, NGOs in CEPRAM, and potential investors that the state was concerned with environmental management. For example, Sectur prioritized the management plan for the Santo Antonio APA because the funding organization (IDB) of a nearby road requested a complete plan before releasing the loan.[25]

The decentralization of APA policy was fundamental in attracting financial resources to APAs. Sectur and Conder attracted funding for APA management plans because they enabled those two agencies to appease lenders, investors, and members of the state environmental council (CEPRAM). The funds invested in APAs by Sectur and Conder were high compared to what the state had invested in environmental

Table 4.5 Funds invested in APA management by the various agencies

Government agency	Amount invested in APA management (US$ 1,000)
Conder*	3,271
CRA†	100
Sectur‡	14,080

*Values for the years 1995 to 1998. *Source:* Tri-annual report 1995–1997 and Annual Report 1998 of Conder (Conder, 1997; Conder, 1999).

†Total values for the years 1995, 1996, and 1997. *Source:* Tri-annual Report 1995–1997 (CRA, 1997). CRA had mostly used its own personnel for APA management. The value above includes only discriminated items in the budget.

‡Total values between 1995 and July 1999, including planned projects. *Source:* Project list, State Secretariat of Culture and Tourism (Sectur, 1999).

Table 4.6 Management plans for the APAs in Bahia until 1999

Initial Administrator	APAs with management plan		APAs without management plan*	
	Number	Area (% of total)	Number	Area (% of total)
Conder	3	187,000 ha (32.2%)	2	6,822 ha (0.4%)
CRA	2	5,395 ha (0.9%)	6	1,231,847 ha (96.2%)
Sectur	7	388,377 ha (66.9%)	1	34,600 ha (2.6%)
Municipalities	0	0,0	6	9,400 ha (0.8%)
Total	**12**	**580,872 ha**	**15**	**1,282,669 ha**

Source: CRA, 1999 and personal consultation with CRA employees.

*Includes management plans whose elaboration is in progress. The Pratigi and Recife das Pinauas APAs were not included in the calculation because they were undefined.

management in the past. The financial resources from development-oriented agencies boosted the establishment of APAs. It was very unlikely that CRA could have attracted the amount of resources raised by the two development agencies. Thus, the decentralization of policy implementation to nonenvironmental agencies can provide significantly more resources than environmental agencies in general, even when those resources mean relatively small percentages of their budgets for development projects.

4.5.3 Competition among Governmental Agencies Can Improve Institutional Capacity

When several governmental agencies are in charge of the implementation of the same policy, there can be a beneficial competition and a synergy created. When nonenvironmental agencies need to implement environmental policies, they have to increase their institutional capacity in the environmental area. At the same time, the environmental agency tends to strengthen its institutional capacity to policy implementation in order to show to policymakers that they are able to be in charge of the policy. In the end, a cycle of increasing capacity building in the public sector can be generated.

To implement the new task of administrating APAs, agencies invest in training, equipment, new personnel, and outside consulting. Agencies invested in equipment for doing the APA job, including office equipment for performing technical studies and facilities and vehicles for doing fieldwork and maintaining and enforcing APAs. Conder and Sectur acquired computers for imaging APA areas. Conder also invested in equipment for managing solid waste in the Northern Coast APA (Conder, 1999). CRA, with its limited resources, had worked with Conder and the Brazilian state oil company (Petrobras) to acquire equipment for collecting waste in the communities and on the beaches of Mangue Seco APA.[26]

Agencies hired or allocated employees to do APA work. Different strategies were used to increase the number of employees working on APAs: hiring new employees, transferring some from other sectors to APA work, incorporating employees from overseas development agencies, or even requesting employees from other government bureaus.[27]

Conder grouped employees from different sectors to work on APAs. For example, the head of the Northern APA project was transferred from a government agency newly merged with Conder. Conder also relied on officials from the English Overseas Development Agency (ODA), which worked on the Northern APA project for more than three years. Sectur also combined officials from different sections with experience in physical and environmental planning, some from a quasi-state tourism bureaucracy, Bahiatursa.

To pursue environmental concerns and promote ecotourism, Sectur created an internal environmental department. Some personnel with experience in environmental issues moved to the new department, others were trained, and external consultants were also hired to elaborate the management plans. The new department oversaw the choice of consultants and supervised their work. Its main job was to work with local interests to ensure implementation of the APAs.

CRA had assigned a small group to work part-time on APAs since the early 1990s, but it did not produce a plan until pressured by other agencies to do so. CRA employees were upset to learn that other agencies would create and administer APAs—they wanted to show that they could do so. CRA allocated several employees to work on APAs, some part-time and some full-time, and hired 43 new employees in 1999, many of whom had been involved with APAs.

Officials in all three agencies were eager to show that they were doing a good job with their APAs, and that they could do as well or better than the other organizations. In developing the management plans for Northern Coast APA and Mangue Seco APA, both Conder and CRA claimed they were pioneers in creating effective management plans on schedule. Officials mentioned activities they had or would pursue with their APAs that other agencies were not pursuing.

CRA officials highlighted their significant efforts to elaborate their first APA management plan (Mangue Seco APA) and their ability to do a good job despite having fewer resources for hiring outside consultants as better funded agencies could do. Although CRA struggled to finish the management plan for the Mangue Seco APA because it lacked resources, the effort showed state authorities and other agencies that it could do the job. The transfer of all APAs to CRA administration in 1999 was viewed as a great victory for CRA employees, and with certain frustration by officials in other organizations, who had expected to administer their own APAs. This transfer allowed CRA to justify an increase of 43 employees.

All the agencies made significant efforts to improve their institutional capacity to deal with APAs. The decentralization of APA policy implementation to several agencies led to a positive competition. Competition among the three agencies prompted them to improve their institutional capacity, thus increasing the overall ability of state organizations to create and administer protected areas. They also interacted with each other improving the flow of information and generating mutual learning.

4.5.4 Getting Local Support: APAs as Potential Investment Magnets

Local governments and other important local actors in developing countries tend to be skeptical about environmental policies from higher government levels because they see those policies as interfering with their jurisdiction and a restriction to economic and social development. This is particularly evident when those policies come from environmental agencies, which are often associated with command-and-control interventions. However, local actors can give more support to environmental policies when they are associated with other development initiatives, such as tourism development, especially when development-oriented agencies are implementing those policies.

The association of APAs with state development agencies and the prospect of attracting state and private investment eased the resistance of local governments to interfere in environmental and land-use matters. Development agencies also spurred the improvement of local environmental organizations and raised environmental consciousness among local development actors (such as landowners) while publicizing APAs and the importance of environmental protection for tourism development.

The creation of an APA by the state interfered with municipal jurisdiction over land use. Control over land matters were some of the most powerful political tools local politicians have at their disposal. Although most municipalities in Bahia did not have the institutional capacity to create or implement land-use management plans,[28] the state had never before intervened substantially in land-use matters.

Although APAs allowed the state to define land-use rules, many local governments regarded them as an opportunity to attract public or private investment, especially for tourism development, rather than as interference in municipal matters. This view resulted from the association of some APAs with the State Secretariat of Culture and Tourism (Sectur), and with Conder, which provided urban infrastructure. The fact that many APAs were created in areas with state infrastructure investments, such as the Green Line Road in the Northern Coast APA and the Ilheus-Itacare Road in the Itacare APA, also suggested that protected areas could attract more public and private investment.

To encourage municipal support for APAs, state agencies organized public hearings to gather information for APA management plans and explain aspects of land use and environmental protection. These efforts to establish APAs and link environmental preservation with tourism development prompted many municipalities (such as Porto Seguro and Cairu) to create or upgrade their institutional structure for environmental protection by creating municipal agencies, passing new legislation, and introducing environmental programs. Such efforts not only indicated to state and federal agencies that the local government was prepared to receive investments in tourism and could manage some decentralized environmental responsibilities. They also allowed municipalities to apply for funds for environmental protection from state, federal, nongovernmental, and international sources.[29] For example, Porto Seguro, which received one of the largest slices of public investment in tourism in the last decade (Bahia State Government, 1997), used the funds to create an environmental agency and to plan several environmental programs (Tosato, Maia, & Braga, 1997).

Local landowners tended to be antagonistic to land-use rules that limit development, such as APA guidelines. However, some landowners seemed to have changed their attitude since the creation of APAs and the promotion of ecotourism by state agencies, especially Sectur. The idea that undeveloped land could be an asset, and that tourism could be promoted with only modest investment, converted landowners to be more supportive of environmental issues. For example, landowners backed the creation of the Itacare APA, hoping that infrastructure investments would attract tourists, and 33 of them proposed several other environmental projects (Newspaper article, n.d.). Many of these landowners had produced cacao for generations using an ecologically friendly method (Conservation International, 1995).[30] Although this approach preserved most of the region's forests, a crop disease devastated the regional economy in the 1980s, and ecotourism appeared to be an important economic alternative.

The involvement of development agencies in APAs seemed to have built local support for environmental protection. Development agencies publicized APAs, trained local officials and citizens, and spread the idea of ecotourism. Before the 1990s, environmental matters were addressed mostly by the environmental agency, which usually used police power and rarely attracted state resources to municipalities. The participation of development agencies changed local conceptions of environmental conservation. Local people began to associate APAs with state resources and opportunities for economic development, thus easing local resistance to state interference in local land-use matters.

Therefore, the decentralization of the implementation of environmental policies to nonenvironmental agencies tends to bring the support of local actors, especially local governments and business interests. They associate environmental policies as development opportunities in other spheres (economic and social), and less as an interference from higher levels of government.

4.6 THE "BAHIAN MODEL":
HORIZONTAL DECENTRALIZATION WITH
CHECKS AND BALANCES

The involvement of development-oriented agencies in environmental policy implementation can certainly generate institutional, financial, and political support for environmental policies, as this case shows. However, such involvement could potentially also generate institutional problems. In the case of Bahia, most of those problems did not arise for several reasons.

One such problem is that development-oriented agencies generally have specific priorities, such as agriculture or tourism development, and environmental objectives may conflict with them. Development-oriented agencies might be tempted to simply neglect environmental concerns while achieving other objectives. However, in Bahia, development agencies established and implemented protected areas as environmental safeguards to gain approval for their development projects from state and external actors. For example, the State Secretariat of Culture and Tourism (Sectur) established many APAs as environmental safeguards for its infrastructure projects financed by international donors. Such protected areas included Santo Antonio APA, which is part of the environmental safeguard for a road financed by the IDB. APAs were also important elements in these agencies' strategies to attract private investments in low-density nature-based tourism. APAs were a guarantee to investors that the state would control chaotic development and land subdivision. Sectur highlighted this point in several brochures for investors (Bahia State Government, 1997). Thus, the establishment of APAs was compatible with the primary objectives of development agencies.

A second challenge is that development projects that depend on environmental safeguards might be controlled by the same agency, which may generate internal conflict—a case of the "foxes guarding the chicken coup." Agencies may prioritize development objectives and disregard proper environmental standards. However, this could be avoided by allowing an outside organization to oversee environmental guidelines and ensure their compatibility with development projects. In Bahia, besides the external actors (donors, the Bank of the Northeast, and the federal government), the state environmental agency (CRA) and environmental council (CEPRAM) acted as independent overseers. Although other agencies also administered APAs, CRA had jurisdiction over environmental offenses, according to the Bahian constitution. Also, all APAs and development projects with significant environmental impacts needed the approval of CRA and CEPRAM. With environmental NGOs comprising one third of its members, CEPRAM could possibly question and bar any action considered deleterious to the environment. Even though my field research did not detect any signs of corruption and policy implementation was also overseen by official accounting organizations, additional oversight by other independent agents could reinforce checking mechanisms and ensure transparent policy implementation.

Moreover, the new task of environmental protection introduced into development agencies unprecedented environmental values and procedures, changing the way the agencies think about and perform their development job. Forming a group of staff members to work on environmental issues created a constituency for environmental protection in internal debates. This contrasted with the usual mode in which development agencies argue against external officials in charge of environmental protection. The staff working on environmental issues within the development agencies showed great commitment to environmental values. A number even risked their jobs and careers to defend proposed environmental guidelines in internal debates. These employees conveyed their knowledge to other staff members or applied it to other projects implemented by the agency.[31] For example, some members of Conder's staff working on the Northern Coast APA contributed their experience in environmental planning to urban development projects.

Third, assigning responsibility for protected areas to several agencies could dissipate scarce organizational and financial resources for implementing them. The same resources concentrated in one agency might generate stronger institutional capacity, particularly when resources come from a dedicated source, such as a new state fund for an environmental program. But in the case of Bahia, financial and organizational resources for environmental protection were not determined a priori like the annual state budget. Public agencies could draw on diverse sources of funding and staff for implementing their policies, thus expanding the total resources devoted to APAs. Indeed, CRA alone would not have been able to establish many APAs because the agency was unlikely to secure the needed substantial increases in budget and staff. Conder and Sectur, in contrast, acquired funds for APAs from their own budgets. These resources substantially expanded the funding the state dedicated to environmental protection.

Fourth, competition among public agencies could generate feuds over public activities and resources. Environmental projects tend to attract funding from international donors and governments and can bring political leverage in requesting and receiving resources. Competing agencies could try to sabotage other agencies' environmental projects or block them politically. In Bahia, competition for controlling APAs was intense among the three public agencies, but sabotage and political blockage did not occur. CRA's top bureaucrats supported the idea of decentralizing APA administration from the beginning, as they realized they would not have the political and financial resources to negotiate with developers and establish a large number of APAs. At first, mid-level bureaucrats in different agencies did show a certain level of mistrust regarding the technical aspects of APAs. However, this mistrust dissipated over time as there was enough work for all the agencies, and they began to cooperate in establishing new APAs. For example, CRA and Conder worked together to develop the management plan for Tinhare-Boipeba APA. The experience Conder acquired in developing the management plan for the huge Northern Coast APA was essential in helping CRA officials create the plan for Boipeba APA. In addition, competition among agencies ended up expanding the overall institutional capacity and financial resources of APAs because agencies wanted to create and manage APAs well in order to gain political leverage in requesting more state funding.

Fifth, dispersion of responsibility for the same task among several agencies might cause confusion about who should do what and when, and also undermine accountability. One agency might expect another agency to do a job assigned to both of them; in the end, no agency would perform the task or assume responsibility for nonperformance or failure. Conflicts could result once agencies started to blame each other. The cases in this study provided some evidence of such conflicts. Conflicts over institutional responsibility for APAs occurred mostly among state agencies, between the executive and judiciary branch, and between state and municipal governments (Puppim de Oliveira & Ogata, 1998). The Abaete APA illustrated these three kinds of conflicts. In a contested development project, the municipal government issued a permit without consulting either CRA or Conder, which had to approve any project located in an APA. Those state agencies, in turn, did not work together to enforce APA guidelines and thus stop the project. In the end, a public prosecutor (similar to a U.S. district attorney) sued both state agencies, the municipal government, and the developer (Ministério Público Federal, Procuradoria da Bahia, 1997).

However, although such conflicts did occur in creating APAs and their guidelines, these disputes are not unique to APAs or protected-area policy. In the environmental arena in Brazil, rules and responsibilities are in transition, and conflicts among diverse public organizations are common in Bahia and other states. In Rio de Janeiro, for example, state and municipal governments blamed each other for water pollution on the beach of Ipanema. State authorities pointed out that the pollution was caused by a leak from the sewer system, which was managed by the municipal government. Municipal officials, in turn, blamed officials of the state-managed sewage treatment facility for lacking the capacity to process large volumes of sewage during heavy rains. There was no agreement about who was responsible for the problem (Jornal do Brasil, 2000).

In sum, the story at the state level examined in this section shows how decentralization of APA policy implementation among state environmental and development agencies enhanced the political clout and resources accruing to APAs in Bahia. Had APAs been concentrated in the hands of the environmental agency, it might not have obtained those resources and overcome the political obstacles.

5

Lessons for Policy Studies

5.1 LEARNING FROM THE RESEARCH:
A NEW FRAMEWORK OF ANALYSIS

This research has attempted to understand policy implementation in developing countries using the case of environmentally protected areas (APAs) in Bahia, Brazil. An analytical framework was developed based on the four main obstacles to establishing protected areas identified by the literature: lack of political support, lack of funding, lack of institutional capacity, and resistance of local actors. Environmental policies usually have little political support in developing countries, where social and economic development has the priority in the government agenda. Even in cases an environmental policy becomes a priority, funding might be a problem, because of governments' tight budgetary constraints, especially in areas not directly linked to economic development objectives. Even when funds are available, governments may lack the institutional capacity to use them effectively because of the lack of personnel, coordination, expertise, or equipment. Finally, local actors can block the implementation of environmental policies if they perceive those policies as going against local interests, as many environmental policies may actually restrict local economic activities. These four obstacles are the basis of the analytic framework developed in this book. In order to design effective policies, policymakers should understand the obstacles to policy implementation and how to overcome them by creating political, financial, and institutional support at several levels of governments as well as in the private sector and civil society. Thus, the policy process should be understood as a whole piece from elaboration to implementation because many policies may sound good for policymakers but not be viable in the implementation stage. The framework developed here can help the assessment of potential problems, and as the case shows, it is possible to build support to overcome obstacles when implementation is decentralized to development-oriented agencies.

The analytical framework developed in this research is primarily relevant to developing countries. I identified four constraints to the implementation of environmental policies: lack of political support at the central level, lack of financial resources, lack of institutional capacity, and resistance at the local level. Although these constraints could exist in any context, they express themselves differently in developed countries. The research helps to reinforce the need to differentiate the literature and analytical frameworks of policy implementation between developed and developing countries.

For example, the lack of institutional capacity is a crucial constraint on policy implementation in many developing countries, especially with regard to equipment and human resources. This problem is less relevant in more developed countries, which tend to have stronger institutional capacity and more financial resources. Although some environmental policies in developed countries are restrained by lack of financing funding is more problematic in poor countries.

The nature of political support for environmental policies also has different dynamics in diverse contexts. In developed countries, political deadlocks can occur when lobbyists try to block implementation of environmental policy. Opposing pro- and anti-environmental forces often battle. In developing countries, political problems result from a lack of environmental policies on the political agenda at all. Thus, the framework for this research can be used to identify constraints on policy implementation, but it must be adapted to a specific context, such as international environmental policies, or local environmental policies in developed countries.

5.1.1 Learning from the Case: How to Overcome the Four Obstacles

Horizontal decentralization, i.e., the involvement of several state agencies in APA administration, helped to overcome the four obstacles described in the analytical framework. Thus, the state government was able to establish several protected areas within about a decade. The traditional strategy of using only heavy-handed command-and-control regulations may be limited. Environmental agencies should be more active in helping others to implement policies. Policymakers should create an institutional system throughout the government structure that generates institutional, financial, and political support for environmental policies.

Tourism projects triggered the involvement of key state agencies in the creation and administration of protected areas in Bahia. At the beginning of the 1990s, the Green Line Road and state tourism program reinforced the state's commitment to tourism as a priority in its economic development strategy. With ecotourism in vogue, and pressures from local and external actors, state authorities created several protected areas in places already affected by tourism and in regions with tourist potential.

The state environmental agency (CRA), which might have been viewed as the natural administrator of protected areas, had little institutional capacity or experience with them by the time the policy started. Thus, development-oriented agencies—the Company for the Development of the Metropolitan Region (Conder) and the State Secretariat of Culture and Tourism (Sectur)—had a window of opportunity to step in and establish protected areas on their own. Since protected areas offered the environmental safeguards required for some tourism projects, agencies created APAs as a way to control decisions concerning these projects. In so doing they hoped to minimize unexpected delays caused by environmental concerns and the bureaucratic procedures of other agencies. Protected areas also offered a chance to grab some political turf, since with more projects in their portfolio, agencies had the leverage to acquire additional financial and institutional resources.

My research identified the four main obstacles to implementation of protected-area policy, all overcome in the Bahia case. As Chapter 4 explains, the decentralization of APA policy among several agencies—especially CRA, Conder, and Sectur—generated institutional, financial, and political support for implementing this policy, which suggests some general lessons about environmental policy implementation. First, because public agencies depended on each other for approval of both APAs and development projects, they could minimize opposition and foster mutual political support at the state level for the establishment of APAs. As a result, the number of APAs created was significant. Thus, creating an institutional environment where agencies work independently but politically supporting each other is crucial in order to remove political obstacles to implement environmental policies. Agencies need to perceive that the good implementation of the policy by other agencies would be important to keep the support for the whole policy across agencies, including their own policy implementation.

Second, the involvement of development agencies, which generally had more funds available for projects, injected considerable state financing into implementating APAs. The amount of funding contributed by development agencies to protected areas was considerably higher than the total the state had previously invested in environmental protection. If APAs had been concentrated in the state environmental agency (CRA) from the beginning, that agency would have been unlikely to raise enough funding and develop the institutional capacity to implement all the APAs. Therefore, new environmental policies should be also in the hands of agencies that hold strong political support, financial resources and institutional capacity to have a good likelihood of taking care of implementation successfully. At the same time, environmental agencies should gradually build capacity of overlooking the implementation process and possibly taking over the task in the future.

Third, state agencies had to increase their institutional capacity rapidly to handle the new task of administering APAs and obtain approval for them from the state environmental council (CEPRAM). The fact that CEPRAM had to approve development projects eased the resistance of environmentalists to allow such projects in protected areas. The approval process certified development agencies' ability to work with APAs and gave them leverage in establishing more APAs. This process generated competition among agencies for improving their institutional capacity to bid for more APAs. The increase in the institutional capacity to implement policies can be done by the establishment of incentives to build capacity among different agencies in order to handle alternative new tasks and sources of funding.

Fourth, the expectation of potential benefits from tourism and public projects associated with APAs eased the resistance of local actors to establishing protected areas. It is doubtful that CRA acting alone to promote such areas solely on the need to protect the environment, would have convinced local governments and landowners to give up some of their development rights. Environmental policies that constrain development rights should be complemented by a system of incentives to bring the political support of local actors; if not, they can perceive the policies as outside interference in their local matters. They should realize that environmental policies can bring short-term and long-term economic and political benefits.

5.2 LESSONS FOR THE CLASSICAL POLICY IMPLEMENTATION LITERATURE

This study was influenced by, and could be included in, some of the classic implementation literature described in chapter 2. As in the third generation of the implementation literature classified by Goggin et al. (1990), this work identifies the key factors that were important in explaining implementation using the case of APA policy in Bahia. These factors were then combined to create an analytical framework that was used to understand the cases of policy implementation. Also, as some of the latest literature on developing countries shows, implementation analyses were based on cases where policy implementation actually was carried out with relative success (Tendler, 1997; Grindle, 1998).

Policy studies tend to make divisions and privilege different frameworks and certain schools of thought, which make it hard to determine what are the best solutions between two conflicting options, such as between quantitative and qualitative research, centralized and decentralized organizations, and top-down and bottom-up approaches. There is a tendency to make Manichaean divisions because of ideologies or analytical shortcomings. Policy analysts and policymakers tend to choose as an analytical framework only one of the possibilities, but detailed empirical studies have shown that the extreme positions in the analyses do not hold in practice.

This research can contribute to the debate between top-down versus bottom-up approaches to implementing policy. Reflecting the trend of the debates, the evidence in this research supports the claim that implementation requires components of both approaches (Najam, 1995). In Bahia, for example APA policy had a strong top-down component early on, when state agencies played a key role in promoting the establishment of APAs. At the same time, bottom-up actions also influenced policy implementation, especially at the local level, even in the beginning. For instance, the idea of creating APAs at the state level to mitigate the impact of development projects began with discussions at the local level, when a development project in Guaibim resulted in the idea of the creation of the Guaibim APA. In another case, in the

Tinhare-Boipeba APA, the local government pursued the enforcement of APA guidelines on its own initiative and without much interference from state agencies. As these two examples in Bahia show, many policies that start as or look like straight top-down implementation are actually a combination of both approaches.

This book also shows there is little practical use for the different types of decentralization identified in the literature. The main authors of that literature tend to categorize decentralization into various types, including deconcentration, devolution, fiscal decentralization, and privatization (Rondinelli, 1981; Rondinelli & Cheema, 1983; Manor, 1999). However, these categories do not shed light on how decentralization actually occurs, and on how it makes policy implementation more effective. Indeed, many cases, including the one in this study, combine all types of decentralization defined in the literature.

APA policy in Bahia encompassed degrees of horizontal decentralization, deconcentration, devolution, and privatization. The state government authorized several state agencies to establish APAs (horizontal decentralization). In turn, these agencies created local branches to execute some tasks (deconcentration), planned to transfer some enforcement responsibility to municipal actors (devolution), and hired some consultants and companies to perform other tasks (privatization). At the same time, a centralized system of checks and balances provided oversight for the whole process. Thus, rather than promoting decentralization for its own sake, analysts must go beyond theoretical definitions to learn what works based on empirical results.

The compartmentalization of responsibilities and tasks among different government agencies is difficult to make as well. The policy process has several integrated spheres (economic, environmental, social) that require different tasks, like the pieces of a puzzle, to deliver effective results. It is unlikely that a coordination mechanism could bring multiple actions from different agencies in a timely manner in a real situation. The policy environment is always changing, and policy analyses find it difficult to anticipate every detail for the future. Agencies should not only have a main responsibility (e.g., environmental protection or tourism development), but also be able to implement other tasks by themselves or to work with other agencies throughout the implementation process. A good example of such complementarity is the implementation of protected areas by tourism development agencies in Bahia.

Finally, the policy process is often fragmented in diverse stages, such as policy making, elaboration, policy implementation, and policy evaluation. This happens both in theory and practice. In theory, different literatures discuss the different processes (Picciotto, 2003, Sabatier, 1986; Pressman and Wildavsky, 1973). In practice, different spheres of the state or government are in charge of different stages of the policy process. For example, the congress passes a law, but the executive has to implement this law. Those that are involved in the policy elaboration may not know the process of policy implementation. Policymakers tend to ignore how policies are going to be implemented later on. Actors involved in the policy implementation may not influence policymaking. When problems happen in policy implementation, it may be too late or difficult to fix them without influencing policy making. Policy process should be regarded as a whole process of analysis and involvement of stakeholders. Stakeholders involved in policy implementation and evaluation should be involved in policymaking. On the other hand, policymakers should know more about policy implementation. The framework of analysis in this book can be a tool for policymakers to integrate policy implementation at the beginning of the policy process.

5.3 INTEGRATING ECONOMIC DEVELOPMENT AND ENVIRONMENTAL PROTECTION IN THE PUBLIC SECTOR

The role of the public sector in controlling development has been essential. On the one hand, governments must react to private demands for investment in infrastructure and public utilities, because in many countries, including Brazil, provision of at least some utilities is within the government sphere. Utilities may include roads, airports, water treatment plants, sanitation, electricity, and telecommunication projects. In Bahia, various state and municipal development agencies were pursuing a series of infrastructure projects to foster tourism development on the coast.

On the other hand, government agencies must create and enforce rules for the use of environmental resources through land-use regulations, construction licenses, and projects that conserve fauna and flora—efforts that sometimes conflict with developmental projects, which may have the potential to cause serious environmental damage. In Bahia, the State Environmental Agency (CRA) was responsible for enforcing compliance, which sometimes conflicted with development interests in the tourism sector.

How can governments handle and integrate these two mandates? This book offers some clues. The main one is the need to integrate environmental concerns with mainstream development discourse and practice in government. Environmental protection and economic development cannot oppose each other. The development process should integrate those apparently confronting objectives. In practice, integration means that development-oriented agencies should handle environmental protection and similarly that environmental agencies should not only enforce command-and-control regulations but also work together with development actors to find the best way to integrate environmental protection and socioeconomic development. In the case of Bahia, environmental protection was a key aspect of the state strategy of tourism development, at least in theory. To acquire the political, financial, and institutional support to implement environmental policies, these policies had to be compatible with development objectives so development agencies would help to implement them.

But how is this possible? How did it happen in Bahia? Four basic factors explain the involvement and interest of development agencies in pursuing environmental policies in Bahia: market pressure, pressure from civil society and external actors, bureaucratic maneuvering, and financial incentives.

First, the marketplace for nature-based tourism and related investments had grown dramatically. Development agencies knew about this growth and created a strategy based on designing projects to attract investments in this sector. Environmentally protected areas were an important part of this strategy. For example, Sectur advertised APAs and their potential for nature-based tourism in brochures distributed to potential private investors (Bahia State Government, 1997). Thus, governments and development agents should integrate environmental objectives with the interests of economic development, showing that environmental protection is a plus (not a minus) for development strategies.

Second, civil society and external actors pressured development agencies to adopt certain environmental safeguards. With the democratization of the country in the 1980s, environmental groups voiced their concerns and pressed development interests to be more environmentally friendly. In Itacare APA, for instance, pressure from local environmental groups changed the design of a sewage treatment plant that would have discharged its waste into a mangrove. International donors and banks were also increasingly requesting environmental guidelines as a condition of loan approval for development projects. Therefore, fostering transparency and integration of different stakeholders in the process can avoid environmental interests being neglected in the agenda of development actors. The integration should be preferably made by someone with enough clout to make development actors listen other stakeholders, as in the case of the state environmental council (CEPRAM).

Third, development-oriented agencies have an interest in keeping environmental matters within their jurisdiction to avoid interference from other agencies. In this case, Sectur decided to retain APAs within its own jurisdiction because several infrastructure projects had APAs as environmental safeguards. Sectur did not want to depend on the state environmental agency to develop APA management plans because CRA could have significantly interfered in the design and schedule of Sectur's projects. As a lesson, governments and development actors should assign some implementation tasks of their environmental policies to development-oriented agencies that have an interest for policies to be implemented in a timely fashion. The transparency and involvement of other stakeholders with decision-making power would help to ensure that those environmental policies were implemented properly.

Fourth, involvement in the environmental "business" can enable an agency to attract funding from diverse government, international, nonprofit, and private sources. In Bahia, Conder received funds from the state treasury to develop the management plan for the Northern Coast APA and from a technical agreement with the English ODA. Putting environmental projects on the agenda of development actors can open up the possibilities of bringing funds from different sources. Many of the development-oriented actors may have the capacity to deviate some funding from "hard" development projects (such as infrastructure) to environmental projects. Those funds may be small compared to the total funds for the development budget, but they could mean a lot for the environmental agenda, which is underfunded in general.

Therefore, integrating environmental protection with a development agenda must entail more than simply promoting economic investment to overcome the point when society can afford environmental amenities, as some economists and proponents of the environmental Kuznets (or inverted U) curve suggest. To foster positive environmental change, governments can "lubricate" the development agenda by establishing incentives for environmental protection and by introducing the political voice of civil society, internal government actors, and external actors in the development process. Creating incentives for government developmental agencies to act in an environmentally friendly manner, as well as opening channels for other voices, are important steps in integrating the two government mandates.

Thus the government policymaking structure is fundamental to effective implementation of a joint mandate. The case study in this book shows that decentralization can help to provide such institutional incentives for integrating environmental protection into the development agenda.

5.4 HORIZONTAL DECENTRALIZATION FOR POLICY IMPLEMENTATION: INCENTIVES WITH CHECKS AND BALANCES

The decentralization of protected-area policy in Bahia was crucial in generating a large number of APAs in the implementation stage. The conditions under which decentralization occurred placed protected areas on the mainstream development agenda. Thus, decentralization created an institutional synergy that generated political, financial, and institutional support for APA policy at the state and local level.

5.4.1 Decentralization without Much Coordination But with Checks and Balances

The case of Bahia offers a different angle on the traditional decentralization-coordination challenge: decentralization without coordination but with incentives and checks and balances. As discussed in Chapter 4, centralizing protected-area policy in the state environmental agency (CRA) would probably have failed because that agency lacked the institutional, financial, and political support necessary to implement the policy. Decentralization involving other state agencies was the alternative.

The involvement of other agencies would, in principle, require some coordination to make sure each agency was fulfilling its role in the implementation process. However, the coordination problem did not undermine policy implementation in the Bahia case. Instead of distributing implementation tasks to different agencies and developing tight, centralized rules, the state government allowed agencies to establish protected areas without much coordination. This eased the implementation process allowing agencies to innovate and retain flexibility. Indeed, coordination was not strictly necessary because tasks were not complementary. Agencies developed the process for establishing APAs almost independently from each other. They could innovate in creating financial and institutional capacity by obtaining funds from different sources and developing the capacity they lacked.

Because of this independent process, state agencies in Bahia took different approaches to developing APA management plans according to their needs and capacities. CRA chose to do most of its work with its own resources and staff because it had limited funds for hiring consultants, and its staff members wanted to show that they could manage the whole process of APA implementation. Conder hired consultants to do the job in-house, so the agency could learn from that experience and add APAs to its portfolio of projects. Conder officials believed that this experience in land-use planning could make it the leading state agency in the APA "business." Sectur hired consulting companies to speed up development of APA management plans because it had a schedule for approving and building infrastructure projects, for which APAs were the environmental safeguards. Thus, lack of coordination did not lead to the lack of implementation but provided agencies with the necessary flexibility to overcome obstacles.

Two factors contributed to effective implementation of APA policy: incentives and checks and balances. First, agencies were motivated to establish protected areas because doing so enabled them to increase their political power and financial resources. Development agencies, in particular, had an incentive to create protected areas to acquire more control over their development objectives, thus avoiding interference from other agencies, especially the environmental agency. Even though these incentives were not *planned*—they were already in place—similar incentives could be created in other institutional settings. For example, a government could make a centralized fund available to any agency involved in implementing certain environmental policies.

Second, in Bahia, a system of checks and balances governed implementation of environmental policy. CEPRAM members and CRA officials had to approve both APAs and development projects, blocking any that did not satisfy certain environmental guidelines. Thus development agencies could not create APAs only on paper; they also had to create APA management plans. Through incentives and checks and balances—which together constituted a carrot-and-stick system—agencies implemented APA policy in a decentralized fashion with minimal need for coordination.

5.4.2 The Forgotten Type of Decentralization: Horizontal Decentralization

This work presents another unusual view of the decentralization puzzle. Implementation of APA policy in Bahia at the state level was conducted mostly through horizontal decentralization—distribution of authority among several agencies at the same governmental level. Such cases are scarce in the decentralization literature. A large part of that literature focuses on *vertical* decentralization—the transfer of authority from central authorities to lower levels of government. Some experts in the field do not even consider horizontal decentralization. For example, my case study would not fit the definitions of decentralization presented by Rondinelli and Cheema (1983) and Manor (1999).

For these authors, true decentralization brings government closer to the population served, as in the case of devolution. This bias seems to result from the context under which the decentralization literature emerged in the 1970s: the failure of large-scale, centralized policies and the rise of democratic movements in many developing countries. The scant attention paid to horizontal decentralization may also reflect the scarcity of examples in the literature and in practice. Cases of horizontal decentralization are often portrayed as agencies squabbling for limited financial and institutional resources (MacKinnon et al., 1986). In the case of Bahia, such infighting did not occur because different decentralized agencies had opportunities to attract resources from different sources.

Horizontal decentralization, indeed, has advantages over both centralized and vertically decentralized structures. Horizontal decentralization entails different dynamics from the most common approaches to vertical decentralization. Although the former does not present some of the supposed benefits of vertical decentralization, such as improved knowledge of local conditions and being close to the population, this research suggests that horizontal decentralization can foster interesting improvements in institutional capacity in developing countries. For example, central governments (in this case, state government) tend to have more financial and human resources compared with local governments. Especially in the environmental field, municipalities often have weak institutional capacity and are unable to implement environmental policies alone. Owing to economies of scale, increasing the institutional capacity of a large number of local governments does not make sense to implement many environmental policies without much central aid. Implementation of APAs requires considerable institutional and financial resources, and municipalities are often unable to implement environ-mental policies alone. (As Table 4.6 shows, none of the municipal APAs had developed a management plan.) What's more, efforts to increase local capacities may not always pay off.

On the other hand, horizontal decentralization also offers some outright advantages over centralized implementation, especially in de-veloping countries where resources are scarce and environmental pro-tection is not generally a priority. For instance, different state government agencies attracted alternative human and financial resources for APA implementation, and the incentives encouraging development agencies to become involved in APA policy helped prevent the traditional po-larization between development and environmental protection. Also, different agencies could innovate and adopt different solutions to imple-ment APAs, increasing their institutional capacity as they faced different problems and exchange experiences. Thus, horizontal decentralization can offer unusual approaches to effective policy implementation that surmount the presumed dichotomy between centralization and vertical decentralization. The system of check and balances is fundamental to make the horizontal decentralization deliver the effective results in policy implementation.

5.5 THE ROLE OF LOCAL ACTORS AND CENTRAL GOVERNMENTS IN DECENTRALIZED POLICY IMPLEMENTATION

Decentralization should not be viewed as simply the complete transfer of responsibilities from central to local governments. It also involves building capacity in the organizations that will perform new tasks—not only in the decentralized organizations but also in the central organi-zation. Central governments have to maintain important roles even as they devolve power (Tendler, 1997), and building capacity for these new roles is necessary. Decentralization must therefore be incremental for all organizations involved, both central and decentralized (Rondinelli & Nellis, 1986). In the Bahia case, central organizations (state agencies) were willing to devolve power to local actors, but could not always create the local institutional capacity needed to transfer responsibilities. State agencies provided some training and information, but they did not offer incentives for local implementation of APA guidelines based on a system of checks and balances.

Central government should play two basic roles in the decentralization process. First, it should create the institutional conditions—including the financial and human resources—decentralized organizations need to perform their new tasks. Central governments should also provide incentives such as fiscal decentralization or funding based on performance. Second, central governments should establish an independent system of checks and balances to oversee the decentralized tasks and provide a mechanism for resolving conflict. This system of checks and balances could be linked to incentives for good performance on decentralized tasks. Conflict resolution is needed in the event of disputes among decentralized organizations and/or clients (the public or firms). In Bahia, the state environmental council (CEPRAM) filled both functions, mostly at the state level. Because they participated in CEPRAM, civil actors such as NGOs and union representatives played a somewhat independent role in settling disputes and overseeing the APA process.

Local governments and nongovernmental groups[1] can often play important roles in designing and implementing policy. However, instead of blindly believing that they can and should be in charge of almost everything, policy analysts must reflect on the institutional limitations of local organizations. The ability of local actors to perform institutional roles depends on the kinds of policies in place and the institutional context in which they occur. In environmental policymaking, local actors can provide essential information and may even prove to be the driving force. For example, in Guaibim APA, locals played an important role in introducing and disseminating the concept of environmentally protected areas statewide. The state used the experience of Guaibim to create other APAs and expand APA policy. The involvement of local actors can also determine the effectiveness of policy implementation. Locals helped establish APA boundaries and the kinds of land use allowed within their borders. Such involvement was essential in motivating local support for enforcing APA guidelines.

However, the role of locals in policymaking is limited by jurisdictions, economies of scale in institutional capacity, and the limitations of local political agendas. For example, in the case of protected areas, local governments cannot create protected areas beyond their political control. At the same time, many of these governments do not have the financial or human resources to sponsor studies to determine which important ecosystems should be protected. Similarly, protected areas may not rank high on municipalities' agendas even though they contain unique and important ecosystems. A more central government confronts fewer policymaking limitations in many cases.

It is in the implementation stage that locals often contribute most to environmental policy. Locals can provide important support such as enforcement, monitoring, and adaptation of environmental policies. For example, in protected areas like the Guaibim APA, locals could make periodic visits, investigate infractions, screen development projects, provide information on environmental quality, and help establish the boundaries of protected areas and their land-use rules. However, the kind of policy and the local institutional context can limit such support. Some local organizations (government or nongovernment) have very limited financial, human, and technical resources to devote to policy implementation. In Bahia, for example, land-use planning, a local responsibility, was barely pursued. Out of more than 400 municipalities, only one, the state capital, had an approved master plan in the end of 1990s, even though the 1988 constitution required all towns over 20,000 inhabitants to have one.

Institutional challenges stemming from the dual governmental mandate also occur at the local level (see the "Integrating Economic Development" section earlier in this chapter). Local governments are in charge of many interventions that affect both economic development and environmental protection. Because of their different institutional contexts, central and local governments have different abilities and incentives to create and implement certain government interventions. Some of the incentives for environmental protection that influence central agencies may not exist at the local level. In the case of Bahia, state (central) development agencies had at least two incentives to establish APAs: the availability of funds for environmental policies, and the opportunity to control environmental issues to avoid interference from other agencies. These incentives were not available to local actors on an ongoing basis.

Many local governments did perceive the creation of protected areas as an incentive to attract public and private tourism investments. This incentive helped state agencies to obtain local political support for creating APAs but not for enforcing or monitoring them, since once the APAs were created (with management plans) and development projects were approved, the incentives ceased to exist. Thus, the creation of more lasting incentives at the local level could foster more local institutional support for implementing environmental policies. For example, the central government could give financial support to local institutions to perform certain enforcement tasks.

In Bahia, state agencies involved municipal governments and non-governmental groups in APA implementation tasks, such as discussion and enforcement of management plans. However, in only a few cases did municipal organizations played the strong role state agencies had expected (Puppim de Oliveira, 2005a). This can be explained by four factors.

First, many municipalities lacked the institutional capacity to perform such tasks. Although state agencies invested in local education, training, and outreach, the practical results often proved disappointing because of the short time frame allowed for such capacity building. Moreover, local governments differ a lot in their capacities. Some local governments, generally larger local governments, have a stronger capacity for policy implementation, and for increasing this capacity, as compared with smaller local governments. This is particularly keen in Brazil, where large parts of the more than 5,500 municipalities do not have, and probably never will because of their size, the capacity to implement most environmental policy implementation tasks. Thus, in a decentralization process, local actors should receive responsibilities gradually and according to their capacity. If they differ in institutional capacity, their responsibility should be different as well. As a result, central governments should also play different roles in policy implementation with different local governments.

Second, municipal organizations had few incentives to engage in capacity building, project screening, and enforcement, as incentives to do so ceased once APAs were created. Therefore, central governments should create incentives to policy implementation as long as they are necessary in order to engage local governments in the process. Because they are different, those incentives can be different as well.

Third, no independent and centralized system of checks and balances tracked the implementation of APA guidelines at the local level. Except for sporadic visits and denouncements, state officials did not monitor environmental quality or the performance of municipal governments in enforcing APA guidelines. Central authorities should create a system of check and balances for local governments, similar to those existing at the state level in Bahia. Responsibility and incentives should be given to locals, but an independent system of checks and balances should monitor the implementation and results in order to gauge changes in policy implementation and incentives.

Finally, many municipal officials are political appointees who can be replaced after elections, so the local government loses much of the enhanced institutional capacity it gains through training and education. Thus, central organizations must drive the decentralization process, continually developing local institutional capacities and providing a system of incentives and checks and balances. The central authorities and external development actors should also focus their capacity to build a more permanent local web of independent professionals and nongovernment organizations.

5.6 LEARNING THE TOUGH REALITY OF THE DEVELOPMENT PROCESS

Debates over sustainable development often raise questions regarding what to preserve, to what extent, by what means, and for whom. In tourism development, these questions are particularly important, because tourism depends on a region's social and environmental assets and conflicts often arise over them. How can countries and localities balance environmental and economic development objectives in this arena?

Or to ask the question more precisely for this case study: Did tourism help protect the environment? There is no clear answer. This research did not assess whether tourism can protect the environment. Such an assessment would be difficult to perform properly. First, no comprehensive data are available to thoroughly evaluate environmental change over time in regions with APAs. Second, even if such data were available, determining causality between environmental protection and tourism development would be difficult. In many areas, tourism is one among many activities taking place. What can be said is that a win–win link between tourism and environmental protection can overcome political, financial, and institutional obstacles to policies like those that create protected areas.

Are APAs a promising solution for protecting the environment? Many APAs were in fact created to mitigate the environmental impacts of tourism development, such as roads and resort construction. One could argue that if the objective of APAs is to preserve the environment completely, no development project would go forward in the first place. On the other hand, if no development had occurred, APAs probably would not have been created. The existence of development projects was the key factor spurring the creation of APAs as an environmental management tool.

Many of the development projects within APAs had long been planned, and had the support of strong constituencies such as federal, state, and municipal governments as well as the local population. They were likely to be implemented anyway, sooner or later. For example, the Green Line Road had existed on paper for twenty years. The regional tourism plan (Prodetur) was a regional priority and the federal government was distributing resources for it. The idea of creating a series of APAs in the 1990s resulted from these projects. APAs were mainly designed to appease local and external pressures for environmental safeguards for those projects, and to attract a certain niche of private investors (low-density nature-based tourism).

However, many APAs on the Bahian coast were suffering from rapid and chaotic tourism development before the 1990s. Local governments had little institutional capacity to control this development. Before APAs became popular, state governments had limited tools for interfering in private projects in areas already altered, such as those with coconut farms or cattle ranches. Development in certain regions was proceeding at an impressive pace with few environmental controls. Thus, APAs provided a powerful management tool to try to control new as well as old development pressures.

Policymakers in the environmental arena should be realistic about the capacity of environmental policies to change development process. The introduction of environmental policies does not stop certain development processes immediately, as perhaps we would like to if we lived in an ideal world. Environmental policies should be integrated in the development process to make gradual changes over time by increasing institutional capacity and showing the advantages of environmental protection. The changes are like making a turn with a large ship. Positive results can occur over the long term but not all at once. Thus an assessment of the development process and the obstacles to environmental policy implementation is very important. Policies should be designed to surmount the obstacles and steer the development process in a different direction.

5.7 A NEW ROLE FOR ENVIRONMENTAL AGENCIES?

The dominant view of agencies in charge of environmental issues in developing countries is that they lack the institutional, political, and financial resources to fulfill the most basic environmental responsibilities. Governments in these countries are usually under pressure to encourage rapid economic development but also to have tight budgetary control. Environmental issues may appear in government discourse but they are hardly a priority because they must fight for scarce public funds and are not often clearly associated with economic development. Indeed, even developed countries face tremendous obstacles to environmental policy implementation, yet they have much larger financial and institutional capacity to implement policies. In these contexts, surmounting all the obstacles to implementing environmental policy effectively is a formidable challenge.

The Bahian case shows how to place environmental issues on the mainstream political agenda of developing countries. Instead of assigning complete responsibility for establishing APAs to the environmental agency, which would be unlikely to do the job well, the state divided responsibility among several agencies, which could then attract more resources to APAs.

Environmental objectives must be integrated into mainstream development practice. For this to occur, development agencies should be allowed to pursue environmental policies, but with checks and balances. This entails changing environmental enforcement from the old-style environmental "police"—in which environmental agencies bullied and penalized offenders—to technical cooperation and implementation by other actors, both state and nonstate actors.

However, giving discretion over environmental issues to development agencies risks allowing such actors to undermine or neglect these responsibilities—akin to putting the fox in charge of the chicken coup. How can development agencies be prevented from appropriating the environmental agenda? The creation of oversight bodies is one approach. Granting more responsibility for implementing environmental policy to development agencies through decentralization should be followed by establishing more oversight mechanisms. Effective oversight requires clear goals measuring environmental performance and transparency and an independent body composed not only of governmental actors but also of NGOs and the private sector. In the case of Bahia, the state environmental council (CEPRAM) filled this oversight role.

The growth of nature-based tourism helped to link environmental protection with development and spurred environmental management in tourist areas. However, it is naïve to view ecotourism as a panacea for environmental protection in developing countries (Honey,

1999). Nature-based tourism requires the same amount of environmental oversight as other forms of tourism. The difference is the opportunity to identify environment and development as a win–win combination, thus fostering government and nongovernmental support for environmental protection throughout the development process.

If governmental and nongovernmental actors see the environment as an asset to be preserved, they will be more willing to invest political and financial support in preventing environmental destruction. Linking environment and development can also generate financial and institutional resources, especially from agencies associated with tourism development. Once such agencies associate environmental protection with their own success, they become more susceptible to working with local and external environmental actors.

The win–win association of creating protected areas within tourism zones was a key to fostering support for those areas. The example of Bahia shows how tourism can be a tool for overcoming the four obstacles of establishing protected areas in developing countries. The same framework could be used to analyze similar environmental management tools in areas facing tourism development, such as the provision of sewage treatment services and collection of solid waste. These tools can be clearly identified as a win–win situation for tourism (sewage systems can maintain cleaner beaches, for example). However, governments must also establish the institutions for overcoming the obstacles to policy implementation. The experience of Bahia offers some insight into how such governmental institutions can be arranged, but further research is needed to provide clearer policy recommendations.

The Bahian experience was important because it showed that alternative institutional and organizational arrangements for making and implementing environmental policy can work under certain conditions. Perhaps these arrangements are not the usual way many policymakers and planners consider when they think about the "ideal," and sometimes unrealistic, models of institutional structure to cope with environmental problems. In the past, a dichotomy has been created between either (a) strong and centralized environmental agency with money, police power, and a committed and well-paid staff to implement environmental policies or (b) a grassroots, decentralized, and bottom-up system of policy implementation. Reality has shown that in practice those two ideal models are not possible, are too costly, or do not achieve the expected results. Environmental agencies should be an articulator of the environmental interests in the development process. They should divide responsibilities of policy implementation with development actors not only by providing technical cooperation and support but also by establishing a system of checks and balances.

The Bahian solution may not be replicable in every country or region, or even prove to be a long-term alternative in Bahia itself,[2] owing to varying economic, institutional, environmental, and social conditions. However, this book shows that a second-best alternative can work relatively well, even if it is not the model that many planners have in mind. Indeed, the Bahian alternative may be the most effective solution to the environment/development challenge under existing conditions and constraints. The objective of this book was to try to understand one alternative and to provide some insights about applying the lessons of Bahia's experience to other situations.

Notes

ACKNOWLEDGMENTS

1. This book uses some ideas and parts of the text of the works developed by the author earlier (see Puppim de Oliveira 2000, 2002, 2003, 2005a and 2005b). However, it represents several advances in the analyses and lessons from the previous works.

CHAPTER 1

1. From now on, I may refer to Northeast Brazil as the Northeast.

2. The term APA (environmentally protected area, or Área de Proteção Ambiental) was created by Law 6,902 in 1981, which also included the legislative National Environmental Policy of 1981. The National Environmental Council (CONAMA) defined APAs as "areas destined to preserve the environmental quality and natural resources in a certain region in order to improve the quality of life of the local population and to protect regional ecosystems" (resolution number 10, 1988, first article). APAs were also introduced in the regulations of the National System of Conservation Units (SNUC) of 2000. An APA has a special zoning system that defines areas for preservation, tourism development, and other activities. The objective of APAs is to avoid the uncontrolled development of tourism and other economic activities. The zoning is supposedly planned with input from local communities and governments.

3. Bank of the Northeast (Banco do Nordeste) is a government development bank that finances public- and private-sector development projects in the Brazilian Northeast and northern regions of the states of Minas Gerais and Espirito Santo. The bank's headquarters are in Fortaleza (in the state of Ceara), but it maintains branch offices all over the region.

CHAPTER 2

1. This division is not consensual and uniform. For example, some authors do not consider privatization a form of decentralization (Manor, 1999).

CHAPTER 3

1. In the 1960s and 1970s, the deforestation of the Brazilian Amazon was mostly provoked by government investments in infrastructure and agrarian colonization projects (Moran, 1983; Mahar, 1989). In another case, the government-sponsored Sardar Sarovar Project in the Narmada River, India, was considered the cause of huge environmental and social impacts (Fisher, 1995; Morse, 1992; Baviskar, 1995). Governments and multilateral financial institutions, like the World Bank, were often blamed for these environmental "tragedies" (Lutzenberger, 1985).

2. A group of developing countries in Stockholm (1972) argued along the lines of the industrialized nations destroyed their environment to be rich, so why can't we do the same?

3. During this time Brazil was under a military dictatorship (which lasted from 1964 to 1985).

4. Secretaria Especial do Meio Ambiente (SEMA) was under the Ministry of Interior. Later on it became part of the Brazilian Environmental Agency (IBAMA).

5. Article 26 of the Brazilian Federal Constitution of 1988 (Brasil, 1996).

6. The National Environmental Council (Conama) defines national environmental policies through a series of resolutions that are based on federal laws or decrees. For example, Conama specifies the limits allowed for air and water pollutants. It is formed by members of the federal government, representatives from states and municipalities, and civil society, such as NGOs and labor and business representatives from the different parts of the country. It is linked directly to the presidential cabinet.

7. Article 30 of the Brazilian Federal Constitution of 1988, states that municipalities can: (a) legislate over any matter of local interest and (b) supplement federal and state legislation if necessary.

8. According to the terminology used by Brazilian governmental institutions, the term *conservation unit* means any kind of protected area (such as a national or state park, ecological station, or APA). An environmentally protected area (APA) indicates only one specific kind of conservation unit (the kind analyzed in my research).

9. This area was inundated in the 1970s after a dam for Itaipu Hydropower Unit was built.

10. Bananal is the largest fluvial island in the world. Today, it is protected under the Araguaia National Park created in 1980.

11. These three kinds of areas could also be created by state or municipal governments.

12. Biological reserves are areas of restricted entrance, used mainly for protecting certain fauna and flora.

13. Biological stations were created to protect samples of certain ecosystems for ecological studies.

14. These categories consist of ecological stations; ecological reserves; environmentally protected areas (APAs); national, state, and municipal parks; biological reserves; national, state, and municipal forests; natural monuments; botanic gardens; zoos; and forest gardens (WWF, 1994).

CHAPTER 4

1. The research was developed using the methodology of case studies (Yin, 1994; Stake, 1995; Ragin and Becker, 1992) by collecting quantitative and qualitative information together and conducting open-ended interviews with personnel in governmental, nonprofit and private organizations involved with tourism and environmental decision making in the Brazilian northeastern region, particularly Bahia state. The research was divided into three stages. First, I collected data and conducted interviews in Brasilia and Salvador, the capital of Bahia, where the headquarters of most state and federal agencies are located and some of the key actors in the environmental arena and tourism sector work. Second, I selected seven case studies of environmentally protected areas (APAs) for in-depth analysis based on the information collected in Salvador. Those APAs were: Guaibim, Itacare, Santo Antonio, Abaete, Mangue Seco, Tinhare-Boipeba, and Northern Coast (respectively numbers 4, 3, 20, 1, 2, 5, and 8 in Figure 4.5). Third, for the in-depth studies of the selected APAs, I moved to the specific regions to complete interviews and data collection with local actors. I conducted more than 160 interviews (varying from 20 minutes to 2 hours) between 1998 and 2005.

2. SUDENE was closed down by a former Brazilian president (Fernando Henrique Cardoso) under the allegation of widespread corruption.

3. Many coastal ecosystems, such as dunes and mangroves, are officially protected under the Brazilian federal constitution. However, because of the lack of proper enforcement mechanisms, developers and squatters have occupied and destroyed part of these ecosystems.

4. In 1993, Brazilian scientists and researchers of the New York Botanical Garden announced that they had found one of the highest tree biodiversity areas in the world during field trip in southern Bahia. More than 450 species of trees were found in one hectare (Conservation International, 1995).

5. Bahia has the longest shoreline in Brazil (approximately 1.18 thousand km). Most of it is formed by mangrove and beautiful beaches with a large potential for tourism.

6. It has government support through links with the Federal Environmental Agency (IBAMA) and the Brazilian state oil company (Petrobras). The Pro-Tamar Foundation has successfully expanded its activities over the years. Today, it acts in several coastal states.

7. Besides Pro-Tamar Foundation, I have identified only two NGOs that operate statewide (Gamba and Germen) through my field research. Of these two, Gamba was more active outside the state and participates in national environmental forums (for instance, Gamba was part of the NGO national network to defend the preservation of the Atlantic Forest).

8. CEPRAM (Conselho Estadual de Meio Ambiente, or State Environmental Council) is a collegiate that decides the most important environmental matters in the state. One third of its members are from governmental agencies, one third are representatives of entrepreneurs and workers, and one third are representatives of environmental NGOs. Any large development project or environmental policy must be approved by CEPRAM in order to be implemented. This kind of environmental council is common in the federal government (CONAMA, Conselho Nacional de Meio Ambiente, or National Environmental Council) and in many Brazilian states. The composition, power, and role of these councils vary according to the state. In some states, as in Bahia, they have very strong roles and significant participation of civil society through environmental NGOs.

9. Article 129, Incision III, of the Brazilian Federal Constitution of 1988 (Brasil, 1996).

10. IBAMA (Instituto Brasileiro do Meio Ambiente e dos Recursos Naturais Renováveis, or Federal Environmental Agency) was in charge of the protected areas under federal jurisdiction. In 2007, IBAMA was divided into two agencies. Chico Mendes Institute, a newly created agency, is in charge of federal protected areas.

11. They remained at the end of the 1990s mostly as they were before. For example, of the 18 parks in the state, only 4 had any management plan in 1999, and two of these were in the hands of IBAMA, the federal environmental agency (CRA, 1999).

12. CRA (Centro de Recursos Ambientais, or Center for Environmental Resources) was the environmental agency of the state of Bahia in charge of enacting and enforcing environmental regulations. It was under the Secretariat of Planning, Science, and Technology (SEPLANTEC) until 2003, when it became part of the newly created Secretariat of the Environment and Water Resources.

13. The Camaçari petrochemical complex is a highly industrialized zone located 60 km from Salvador, Bahia's capital. Some 50 industrial plants produce various kinds of petrochemical products in 2005.

14. Municipal governments are in charge of land-use rules as interpreted by the Brazilian constitution.

15. Such a council would be composed of state and municipal governments and members and organizations of local civil society.

16. Bahiatursa (Bahia Turismo S.A., or the Bahia Tourism Authority) was an agency for the coordination of tourism development. Bahiatursa was in

charge of tourism promotion and planning in the state of Bahia and was linked to the State Secretariat of Culture and Tourism (SECTUR). Bahiatursa changed its name to Empresa de Turismo da Bahia S.A. Sectur became later SETUR (Secretaria de Turismo or Secretariat of Tourism).

17. CONDER (Companhia de Desenvolvimento da Regiao Metropolitana, or Company for the Development of the Metropolitan Region) was the state agency in charge of planning for Salvador, the state capital, and surrounding urban areas. It was under the jurisdiction of SEPLANTEC (Secretariat of Planning, Science, and Technology). Conder changed its name to Companhia de Desenvolvimento Urbano do Estado da Bahia. Later, it became part of the State Secretariat of Urban Development (Secretaria de Desenvolvimento Urbano).

18. The other alternative to create protected areas is through the state legislature, but this was uncommon (e.g., in Bahia all APAs were created by decree). I am talking here about state conservation units. In the case of federal conservation units, the president or congress must issue a federal legislation. In the case of municipal conservation units, the mayor or city council must pass municipal legislation.

19. Before 1990, only two nonenvironmental state agencies—Conder and the state Secretariat of Agriculture (Seagri)—had created conservation units. However, those were in urban areas, such as the Getulio Vargas Zoo and the Abaete Lagoon Park and APA in Salvador (CRA, 1999).

20. Only two conservation units over 2,000 hectare were created before 1990: Gruta dos Brejoes APA (11,900 ha) and Ecological Reserve and Park of Itaparica (CRA, 1999). But no steps were made to implement their management.

21. Several important development projects had been stalled in CEPRAM for environmental approval because of the opposition of environmental organizations. For example, a huge forestry project for the pulp industry called Projeto Vera Cruz in the south of the state was stalled for several years in CEPRAM before it got approved. It was approved after many modifications and a heated debate in CEPRAM.

22. In an informational brochure for foreign investors, Sectur emphasizes APAs as part of the reasons to invest in nature-based tourism in Bahia (Bahia State Government, 1997).

23. According to state law 3858 of November 3, 1988 (Puppim de Oliveira & Ogata, 1998; Governo da Bahia, 1997).

24. The Conder budget for projects in 1998 was US$ 11,710,440. This includes only funding for projects, not including personnel, capital, or other operational expenses (data collected by Conder).

25. For example, Santo Antonio APA was created after Ponta da Baleia APA, but the management plan of the former was made before the latter.

26. This actually was the result of an attempt by Petrobras to improve its image after an offshore oil spill, for which Petrobras was fined.

27. Because firing public employees is difficult, moving employees who are idle in one agency to another is very common in the Brazilian bureaucracy.

28. Out of the 415 municipalities in Bahia only Salvador, the capital, had a municipal master plan in 1998.

29. There were several sources of environmental funding for municipal governments, such as the National Fund for the Environment (Fundo Nacional do Meio Ambiente, or FNMA) from the Federal Ministry of the Environment, Water Resources and the Amazon (Ministério do Meio Ambiente, or MMA), and the Program for Decentralized Implementation (Programa de Execução Decentralizada, or PED) from the state and federal government.

30. Tree shadow is essential for growing cacao, which is planted in the middle of a natural forest.

31. A good example is the environmental zoning learned by Conder staff in the Northern Coast APA. The skills were used in other projects (e.g., urbanization and master plans) afterward.

CHAPTER 5

1. When I refer to local actors, or simply locals, I include both local governments and nongovernmental groups.

2. Indeed, all the APAs were put under CRA responsibility in 1999, and later on, the newly established Secretariat of the Environment and Water Resources created a special unit to take care of all protected areas.

Bibliography

A Tarde (1997a, August 2). Óleo polui praias do litoral norte. *A Tarde News-paper.*

A Tarde (1997b, September 9). Associação de moradores em campanha contra loteamento—local. *A Tarde Newspaper.*

A Tarde (1997c, October 23). Ministério Público abre inquérito contra loteamento na Pedra do Sal. *A Tarde Newspaper,* p. 6.

A Tarde (1998, January 19). Manifestantes fazem ato em defesa de dunas. *A Tarde Newspaper,* p. 8.

Agrawal, Arun, & Gupta, Krishna (2005). Decentralization and participation: The governance of common pool resources in Nepal's Terai. *World Development,* 33(7), 1101–1114.

Albers, H. J., & Grinspoon, E. (1997). A comparison of enforcement of access restrictions between Xishuangbanna Nature Reserve (China) and Khao Yai National Park (Thailand). *Environmental Conservation,* 24(4), 351–362.

Alessa, Lilian, Bennett, Sharon M., & Kliskey, Andrew D. (2003). Effects of knowledge, personal attribution and perception of ecosystem health on depreciative behaviors in the intertidal zone of Pacific Rim National Park and Reserve. *Journal of Environmental Management,* 68(2), 207–218.

Almanaque Abril (1995). Volume 1. São Paulo: Editora Abril.

Alderman, Claudia L. (1994). The economics and the role of privately-owned lands used for nature tourism, education and conservation. In Mohan Munasinghe & Jeffrey McNeely (Eds.), *Protected Area Economics and Policy: Linking Conservation and Sustainable Development.* Washington, D.C.: World Bank.

Ames, Barry, & Keck, Margaret E. (1997). The politics of sustainable development: Environmental policy making in four Brazilian states. *Journal of Interamerican Studies & World Affairs,* 39(4), 1–40.

Análise & Dados (1994). Silvicultura e ecologia no extremo sul da Bahia: fatos e crendices. Entrevista com Paulo de Tarso Alvim. *Análise & Dados,* 4(2–3), 108–114.

Anderson, Terry A., & Leal, Donald R. (1992). Free market versus political environmentalism. *Harvard Journal of Law and Public Policy*, 15(2), 297–310.

Angotti, Thomas (2000). Ciudad Guayana from growth pole to metropolis, central planning to participation. *Journal of Planning Education and Research*, 20(3), 329–338.

Arjunan, M., Holmes, Christopher, Puyravaud, Jean-Philippe, & Davidar, Priya (2006). Do developmental initiatives influence local attitudes toward conservation? A case study from the Kalakad–Mundanthurai Tiger Reserve, India. *Journal of Environmental Management*, 79(2), 188–197.

Ayee, Joseph R. A. (1994). *An Anatomy of Public Policy Implementation*. Hants, U.K.: Avebury Ashgate Publishing.

Bahia State Government (1997). *Bahia Tourism Development Program: Investment Opportunities*. Brochure. Salvador: Department of Culture and Tourism.

Bahia State Government (2005). Prodetur-BA. Retrieved January 13, 2005, from Bahia State web site http://www.sct.ba.gov.br/turismo/concluidos_prodetur.asp.

Baker, P. R. (1990). *Tourism and Protection of Natural Areas*. Washington, D.C.: National Park System.

Banco do Nordeste (1996a). *Cadastro do Empreendimento, Prodetur*. Brochure (12/12/1996).

Banco do Nordeste (1996b). *Oportunidades de Investimento: Turismo, Nordeste do Brasil*. Fortaleza, Brazil: Banco do Nordeste.

Banco do Nordeste (1997). Prodetur confirma a presença do Nordeste na expansão do mercado. *Notícias Especial*, p. 12, September.

Banco do Nordeste (2005). Prodetur I. Retrieved January 13, 2005, from the Banco do Nordeste web site http://www.bnb.gov.br/content/aplicacao/PRODETUR/visao/gerados/prodetur_visao_componentes.asp.

Bardach, Eugene (1977). *The Implementation Game: What Happens after a Bill Becomes a Law*. Cambridge, MA: MIT Press.

Barzetti, Valerie (1993). *Parques y Progreso: Areas Protegidas y Desarollo Económico en América Latina y el Caribe*. Gland, Switzerland: IUCN and IDB.

Baviskar, Amite (1995). *In the Belly of the River: Tribal Conflicts over Development in the Narmada Valley*. Delhi, India: Oxford University Press.

Beard, Victoria A. (2002). Covert planning for social transformation in Indonesia. *Journal of Planning Education and Research,* 22(1), 15–25.

Beckerman, W. (1992). Economic growth and the environment: Whose growth? Whose environment? *World Development*, 20(4), 481–496.

Bennet, Robert J. (1990). *Decentralization: Local Governments, and Markets. Towards a Post-Welfare Agenda*. Oxford, U.K.: Clarendon Press.

Berman, Paul (1978). The study of macro and micro-implementation. *Public Policy*, 26(2), 157–184.

Bernardes, Ernesto, & Nanne, Kaike (1994). O Brasil Organizado Funciona. *Veja*, February 9, 70–77.

Boardman, Robert, & Shaw, Timothy M. (1995). Protecting the environment in Indonesia: Policies and programs. In O. P. Dwivedi, & D. Vajpeyi (Eds.), *Environmental Policies in the Third World: A Comparative Analysis*. Westport, CN: Greenwood Press.

Boo, Elizabeth (1990). *Ecotourism: The Potentials and Pitfalls*. Baltimore, MD: World Wildlife Fund.

Bosselman, Fred P. (1978). *In the Wake of Tourism*. Washington, D.C.: Conservation Foundation.

Brandon, K. E., & Brandon, C. (1992). Introduction. *World Development*, 20(4), 477–479.

Brasil (1996). *Constituição Brasileira de 1988* 8th ed. São Paulo: Editora Atlas.

Briassoulis, Helen (1995). The environmental internalities of tourism: Theoretical analysis and policy implications. In Harry Coccossis & Peter Nijkamp (Eds.), *Sustainable Tourism Development*. Brookfield, USA: Avebury Ashgate Publishing.

Brinkerhoff, Derick W. (1996). Coordination issues in policy implementation networks: An illustration from Madagascar's Environmental Action Plan. *World Development*, 24(9), 1497–1510.

Burger, Joanna, & Gochfeld, Michael (1998). Effects of ecotourists on bird behavior at Loxanatchee National Wildlife Refuge, Florida. *Environmental Conservation*, 25(1), 13–21.

Butler, R. (1991). Tourism, environment, and sustainable development. *Environmental Conservation*, 18(3), 201–209.

Buultjens, J., Ratnayake, I., Gnanapala, A., & Aslam, M. (2005). Tourism and its implications for management in Ruhuna National Park (Yala), Sri Lanka. *Tourism Management*, 26(5), 733–742.

Casson, Anne, & Obidzinski, Krystof (2002). From new order to regional autonomy: Shifting dynamics of illegal logging in Kalimantan, Indonesia. *World Development*, 30(12), 2133–2151

Ceballos-Lascurain, Hector (1988). The Future of Ecotourism, *Mexico Journal*, 17 (January), 13–14.

Ceballos-Lascurain, Hector (1996). *Tourism, Ecotourism and Protected Areas*. Gland, Switzerland: World Conservation Union (IUCN).

Centro de Recursos Ambientais (n.d.). *Ações Normativas—CEPRAM*.

CEPRAM, Conselho Estadual de Meio Ambiente (1999). Table with all CEPRAM resolutions between 1990 and 1999.

Chant, Sylvia (1992). Tourism in Latin America: Perspectives from Mexico and Costa Rica. In David Harrison (Ed.), *Tourism and Less Developed Countries*. London: Belhaven Press.

Conder, Companhia de Desenvolvimento da Região Metropolitana (1997). *Relatório de Atividades 1995–1997*. Salvador, Brazil: Conder.

Conder, Companhia de Desenvolvimento da Região Metropolitana (1999). *Relatório Anual*. Salvador, Brazil: Conder.

Conservation International (1995). *The Economics of Biodiversity: Conservation in the Brazilian Atlantic Forest*. Washington, D.C.: Conservation International.

Corte, Dione A. A. (1997). *Planejamento e Gestão de APAs: Enfoque Institucional*. Série Meio Ambiente em Debate, number 15. Brasília, Brazil: IBAMA.

CRA, Centro de Recursos Ambientais (1997). *Relatório de Atividades 1995– 1997*. Salvador, Brazil: CRA.

CRA, Centro de Recursos Ambientais (1999). *Relatório de Atividades 1999*. Salvador, Brazil: CRA.

CRA, Centro de Recursos Ambientais (2004). Retrieved on December 12, 2004, from http://www.cra.ba.gov.br.

De Boer, W. F., & Baquete, D. S. (1998). Natural resource use, crop damage and attitudes of rural people in the vicinity of the Maputo Elephant Reserve, Mozambique. *Environmental Conservation*, 25(3), 208–218.

Dearden, P. (1988). Protected areas and the boundary model: Meares Island and Pacific Rim National Park. *Canadian Geographer*, 32(3), 256–265.

Deng, Jinyang, King, Brian, & Bauer, Thomas (2002). Evaluating natural attractions for tourism. *Annals of Tourism Research*, 29(2), 422–438.

Deroubaix, José-Frédéric, & Lévêque, François (2006). The rise and fall of French Ecological Tax Reform: Social acceptability versus political feasibility in the energy tax implementation process. *Energy Policy*, 34(8), 940–949.

Desai, Nitin (1991). A Development Planner Looks at Environmental Management. In Denizhan Erocal (Ed.), *Environmental Management in Developing Countries*. Paris: OECD.

Desai, Uday (1992). Introduction. *Policy Studies Journal*, 20(4), 621–627.

Desai, Uday (Ed.) (1998). *Ecological Policy and Politics in Developing Countries: Economic Growth, Democracy, and Environment*. Albany, NY: SUNY Press.

Diegues, A.C.S. (1994). *O Mito Moderno da Natureza Intocada*. São Paulo: NUPAUB—USP.

Dubasak, M. (1990). *Wildnerness Preservation: A Cross-Cultural Comparison of Canada and the United States*. New York: Garland Publishing.

Eastmond, Amarella, & Faust, Betty (2006). Farmers, fires, and forests: A green alternative to shifting cultivation for conservation of the Maya forest? *Landscape and Urban Planning*, 74(3–4), 267–284.

Elmore, Richard F. (1979). Backward mapping: Implementation research and policy decisions. *Political Science Quarterly*, 94(4), 601–616.

Fiallo, E.A., & Jacobson, S. K. (1995). Local communities and protected areas: Attitudes of rural residents towards conservation in Machalilla National Park, Ecuador. *Environmental Conservation*, 22(3), 241–249.

Fisher, William F. (Ed.) (1995). *Toward Sustainable Development? Struggling Over India's Narmada River*. Armonk: M. E. Sharpe.

Friedmann, John (1973). *Retracking America: A Theory of Transactive Planning*. Garden City, NY: Doubleday.

Gamman, John K. (1995). *Overcoming Obstacles in Environmental Policymaking: Creating Partnerships through Mediation.* Albany, NY: State University of New York Press.

Gbadegesin, Adeniyi, & Ayileka, Olatubosun (2000). Avoiding the mistakes of the past: Towards a community oriented management strategy for the proposed National Park in Abuja-Nigeria. *Land Use Policy,* 17(2), 89–100.

Goggin, Malcolm L., Bowman, Ann O., Lester, James P., & O'Toole Jr., Lawrence (1990). *Implementation Theory and Practice: Towards a Third Generation.* Glenview, IL: Scott, Foresman.

Goulet, Denis (1989). Participation in development: New Avenues. *World Development,* 17(2), 165–178.

Governo do Estado da Bahia (1998). *APA Itacaré-Serra Grande, Plano de Manejo.* Salvador, Brazil: Bahia State Government.

Grindle, Merilee S. (Ed.) (1980). *Politics and Policy Implementation in the Third World.* Princeton, NJ: Princeton University Press.

Grindle, Merilee (Ed.) (1998). *Getting Good Government: Capacity Building in the Public Sectors of Developing Countries.* Cambridge, MA: Harvard Institute of International Development.

Hannah, L., Rakotosamimanana, B., Ganzhorn, J., Mittermeier, R. A., Olivieri, S., Iyer, L., Rajaobelina, S., Hough, J., Andriamialisoa, F., Bowles, I., & Tilkin, G. (1998). Participatory planning, scientific priorities, and landscape conservation in Madagascar. *Environmental Conservation,* 25(1), 30–36.

Hardi, Peter (1992). *Impediments on Environmental Policy-Making and Implementation in Central and Eastern Europe: Tabula Rasa vs. Legacy of the Past.* Berkeley, CA: University of California.

Harrison, J., Miller, K. R., & McNeely, J. A. (1984). The world coverage of protected areas: Development goals and environmental needs. In J. A. McNeely & K. R. Miller (Eds.), *National Parks, Conservation and Development: The Role of Protected Areas in Sustaining Society.* Washington D.C.: IUCN and Smithsonian Institution Press.

Healey, P. (1997). *Collaborative Planning: Shaping Places in Fragmented Societies.* London: Macmillan Press.

Hibbard, Michael, & Lurie, Susan (2000). Saving land but losing ground: Challenges to community planning in the era of participation. *Journal of Planning Education and Research,* 20(2), 187–195.

Homewood, Katherine M. (2004). Policy, environment and development in African rangelands. *Environmental Science & Policy,* 7(3), 125–143.

Honey, Martha (1999). *Ecotourism and Sustainable Development: Who Owns the Paradise?* Washington, D.C.: Island Press.

Hunter, Colin, & Green, Howard (Eds.) (1995). *Tourism and the Environment: A Sustainable Relationship?* London: Routledge.

IBGE, Instituto Brasileiro de Geografia e Estatística (2005). Censo Demográfico 2000. Retrieved January 15, 2005, from IBGE's Web site: http://www.ibge.gov.br.

IUCN, World Conservation Union (1991). *Parks*, 2 (3), November.

IUCN, World Conservation Union (2003). *Recommendations from the Fifth IUCN World Parks Congress.* Retrieved August 17, 2004 from IUCN web site: http://www.iucn.org/themes/wcpa/wpc2003/index.htm.

IUCN, World Conservation Union & UNEP—United Nations Environment Programme (2003). *United Nations List of Protected Areas.* Cambridge, U.K.: IUCN Publications Service.

Jan, George (1995). Environmental Protection in China. In O. P. Dwivedi & D. Vajpeyi (Eds.), *Environmental Policies in the Third World: A Comparative Analysis.* Westport, CT: Greenwood Press.

Jornal do Brasil (2000, February 2). Língua negra não tem dono. *Jornal do Brasil.*

Kaljonen, Minna (2006). Co-construction of agency and environmental management. The case of agri-environmental policy implementation at Finnish farms. *Journal of Rural Studies*, 22(2), 205–216.

Kamieniecki, Sheldon (Ed.) (1993). *Environmental Politics in the International Arena: Movements, Parties, Organizations and Policy.* Albany, NY: State University of New York Press.

Kamieniecki, Sheldon, Gonzalez, George A., & Vos, Robert O. (Eds.) (1997). *Flashpoints in Environmental Policymaking: Controversies in Achieving Sustainability.* Albany, NY: State University of New York Press.

Kaufman, Herbert (1973). *Administrative Feedback.* Washington D.C.: Brookings Institution.

Klarer, Jurg, & Francis, Patrick (1997). Regional overview. In J. Klarer & B. Moldan (Eds.), *The Environmental Challenge for Central European Economies in Transition*, Chichester, U.K.: John Wiley & Sons.

Landau, Martin (1969). Redundancy, rationality, and the problem of duplication and overlap. *Public administration Review*, 29 (July, August), 346–358.

LaPage, W. F. (1996). America's self-funding park system: The New Hampshire model. In M. Munasinghe & J. McNeely (Eds.) *Protected Area Economics and Policy.* Washington D.C.: World Bank.

Lemos, Maria C. (1998). The politics of pollution control in Brazil: State actors and social movements cleaning up Cubatão. *World Development*, 26(1), 75–88.

Lemos, Maria C., & Oliveira, Joao L. F. (2004). Can water reform survive politics? Institutional change and river basin management in Ceará, Northeast Brazil. *World Development*, 32(12), 2121–2137.

Lipsky, Michael (1980). *Street-Level Bureaucracy.* New York: Russell Sage Foundation.

Llinás, Miguel S. (1996). El espacio turístico y su consumo en la Isla de Mallorca. In Adyr A. B. Rodrigues (Ed.), *Turismo e Geografia: Reflexões Teóricas e Enfoques Regionais.* São Paulo: Editora Hucitec.

Lopes, Ignez V., Bastos Filho, Guilherme S., Biller, Dan, & Bale, Malcolm (Eds.) (1996). *Gestão Ambiental no Brasil: Experiência e Sucesso.* Rio de Janeiro: FGV Editora.

Loureiro, Maria Rita, & Pacheco, Regina S. (1995). Formação e consolidação do campo ambiental no Brasil: Consensos e disputas (1972–92). *Revista de Administração Pública (RAP)*, 29(4), 137–53.

Lu, Yihe, Chen, Liding, Fu, Bojie, & Liu, Shiliang (2003). A framework for evaluating the effectiveness of protected areas: The case of Wolong Biosphere Reserve. *Landscape and Urban Planning*, 63(4), 213–223.

Lutzenberger, Jose (1985). The World Bank's Polonoroeste Project: A social and environmental catastrophe. *Ecologist*, 15(1–2), 69–72.

MacKinnon, J., MacKinnon, K., Child, G., & Thorsell, J. (1986). *Managing Protected Areas in the Tropics*. Gland, Switzerland: World Conservation Union.

Mahanty, Sanghamitra (2002). Conservation and development interventions as networks: The case of the India Ecodevelopment Project, Karnataka. *World Development*, 30(8), 1369–1386.

Mahar, Dennis J. (1989). *Government Policies and Deforestation in Brazil's Amazon Region*. Washington, D.C.: World Bank.

Manor, James (1999). *The Political Economy of Democratic Decentralization*. Washington, D.C.: World Bank.

Mater Natura—Instituto de Estudos Ambientais (1996). *Cadastro Nacional de Instituições Ambientalistas—Ecolista*. Curitiba, Brazil: Mater Natura.

Mathieson, A., & Wall, G. (1996). *Tourism: Economic, Physical and Social Impacts*, 2nd ed. Essex, U.K.: Longman Group.

May, Peter H., & Pastuk, Marília (1996). Turismo e áreas litorâneas: O caso da Bahia. In Ignez V. Lopes et al. (Eds.), *Gestão Ambiental no Brasil: Experiência e Sucesso*. Rio de Janeiro: Editora Fundação Getúlio Vargas.

May, V. (1991). Tourism, environment, and development: Values, sustainability and stewardship. *Tourism Management*, 12(2), 112–118.

Mazmanian, Daniel A., & Sabatier, Paul A. (1983). *Implementation and Public Policy*. Chicago: Scott, Foresman.

McLaren, Deborah (1998). *Rethinking Tourism and Travel*. West Hardford, CT: Kumarian Press.

McNeely, Jeffrey A. (Ed.) (1993). *Parks for Life: Report of the Fourth World Congress on National Parks and Protected Areas. Caracas, Venezuela, 10–21 February 1992*. Gland, Switzerland: World Conservation Union and World Wildlife Fund.

Migdal, Joel S. (1988). *Strong Societies and Weak States*. Princeton, NJ: Princeton University Press.

Ministério do Meio Ambiente (2004). Retrieved on March 2, 2004, from http://www.mma.gov.br.

Ministério Público Federal, Procuradoria da Bahia (1997). *Relatório ao Juiz Federal da 3a Vara Federal da Bahia*. December 12. Salvador, Brazil.

Ministry of Economy, Treasury, and Planning; Bank of the Northeast, & Inter-American Development Bank (1992). *Prodetur-NE: Segmento de Infra-estrutura e Apoio*. Carta Consulta à Cofiex, February.

Moran, Emilio F., editor (1983). *The Dilemma of Amazonian Development*. Boulder, CO: Westview Press.

Morell, David & Poznanski, Joanna (1985). Rhetoric and reality: Environmental politics and environmental administration in developing countries. In H. Jeffrey Leonard (Ed.), *Divesting Nature's Capital. Political Economy of Environmental Abuse in the Third World*. New York: Holmes & Meier.

Morse, Bradford (1992). *Sardar Sarovar: Report of the Independent Review*. Ottawa, Canada: Resources Futures International.

Munasinghe, Mohan (1996). Economic and Policy Issues in Natural Habitats and Protected Areas. In M. Munasinghe & J. McNeely (Eds.) *Protected Area Economics and Policy*. Washington D.C.: World Bank.

Najam, Adil (1995). *Learning from the Literature on Policy Implementation: A Synthesis Perspective*. IIASA Working Paper 95-61. Laxenburg, Austria: IIASA—International Institute for Applied Systems Analysis.

Nash, Roderick (1978). *Nature in World Development: Patterns in the Preservation of Scenic and Outdoor Recreation Resources*. Rockfeller Foundation Working Papers. March.

Nepal, Sanjay K. (2000). Tourism in protected areas: The Nepalese Himalaya. *Annals of Tourism Research, 27*(3), 661–681.

Newspaper article (n.d.). APA tem incremento de ecoturismo, unidentified newspaper article copied in the library of the Bahia Tourism Authority (Bahiatursa), Salvador.

Nogueira Neto, Paulo (1992). *Estações Ecológicas, uma Saga de Ecologia e Política Ambiental*. São Paulo: Empresa das Artes.

NPS, National Park Service (2003a). Economic impacts of national park visitor spending on gateway communities, systemwide estimates for 2001. NPS Systemwide economic impacts, 2001, Final draft, January 2003.

NPS, National Park Service (2003b). Statistical Abstract 2003. Manuscript from NPS.

O Globo (2006, August 8). Operação da PF Prende $1/4$ do IBAMA no Rio. *O Globo*.

Padua, J. A. (1987). Natureza e projeto nacional: As origens da ecologia política no Brasil. In J. A. Padua (Ed.), *Ecologia e Política no Brasil*. Rio de Janeiro: Iuperj.

Palumbo, Dennis J., & Harder, Marvin A. (1981). Introduction. In Dennis J. Palumbo & Harder, Marvin A. (Eds.), *Implementing Public Policy*. Lexington, MA: Lexington Books.

Panayotou, Theodore (1993). *Green Markets: The Economics of Sustainable Development*. San Francisco: ICS Press.

Parry, Taryn R. (1997). Achieving balance in decentralization: A case study of education decentralization in Chile. *World Development, 25*(2), 211–225.

Pearce, David W., & Turner, R. K. (1990). *Economics of Natural Resources and the Environment*. New York: Harvester Wheatsheaf.

Picciotto, Robert (2003). International trends and development evaluation: The need for ideas. *American Journal of Evaluation, 24*(2), 227–234.

Pichon, Francisco J. (1992). Agricultural settlement and ecological crisis in the Ecuadorian Amazon frontier: A discussion of the policy environment. *Policy Studies Journal*, 20(4), 662–678.

Pinto da Silva, Patricia (2004). From common property to co-management: Lessons from Brazil's first maritime extractive reserve. *Marine Policy*, 28(5), 419–428.

Pollard, John, & Rodriguez, Rafael Dominguez (1993). Tourism and Torremolinos: Recession or reaction to the environment. *Tourism Management*, 14(4), 247–258.

Pouliquen-Young, O. (1997). Evolution of the system of protected areas in Western Australia. *Environmental Conservation*, 24(2), 168–181.

Prazan, Jaroslav, Ratinger, Tomas, & Krumalova, Veronika (2005). The evolution of nature conservation policy in the Czech Republic—challenges of Europeanisation in the White Carpathians Protected Landscape Area. *Land Use Policy*, 22(3), 235–243.

Pressman, Jeffrey L., & Wildavsky, Aaron (1973). *Implementation*. Berkeley, CA: University of California Press.

Prefeitura Municipal de Jandaíra (n.d.). *Mangue Seco*. Tourism brochure.

Puppim de Oliveira, Jose A. (2005a). Tourism as a force for establishing protected areas: The case of Bahia, Brazil. *Journal of Sustainable Tourism*, 13(1), 24–49, January.

Puppim de Oliveira, Jose A. (2005b). Enforcing protected area guidelines in Brazil: What explains participation in the implementation process? *Journal of Planning Education and Research—JPER*, 24(4), 420–436, June.

Puppim de Oliveira, Jose A. (2003). Governmental responses to tourism development: Three Brazilian case studies. *Tourism Management*, 24(1), 97–110.

Puppim de Oliveira, Jose A. (2002). Implementing environmental policies in developing countries through decentralization: The case of protected areas in Bahia, Brazil. *World Development*, 30(10), 1713–1736.

Puppim de Oliveira, Jose A., with Camargo, Aspásia and Capobianco, João Paulo (Eds.) (2002). *Meio Ambiente Brasil: Avanços e Obstáculos Pós-Rio-92* (summarized version in English: *The State of the Brazilian Environment: A View from Civil Society*). São Paulo: Editora Estação Liberdade.

Puppim de Oliveira, Jose Antonio (2000). *Implementing Environmental Policies in Developing Countries: Responding to the Environmental Impacts of Tourism Development by Creating Environmentally Protected Areas in Bahia, Brazil*. Doctoral thesis, Department of Urban Studies and Planning, Massachusetts Institute of Technology.

Puppim de Oliveira, Jose A., & Ogata, Maria G. (1998). Análise institucional da gestão e uso do solo nas áreas protegidas no Estado da Bahia. *Análise & Dados*, 8(4), 89–98.

Quintana, Jesus, & Morse, Stephen (2005). Social interactions and resource ownership in two private protected areas of Paraguay. *Journal of Environmental Management*, 77(1), 64–78.

Ragin, Charles C., & Becker, Howard S. (Ed.) (1992). *What Is a Case?: Exploring the Foundations of Social Inquiry*. New York: Cambridge University Press.

Rawat, G. S. (1997). Conservation status of forests and wildlife in the Eastern Ghats, India. *Environmental Conservation*, 24(4), 307–315.

Reich, Michael R., & Bowonder, B. (1992). Environmental policy in India strategies for better implementation. *Policy Studies Journal*, 20(4), 643–661.

Rein, Martin, & Rabinovitz, Francine F. (1977). *Implementation: A Theoretical Perspective*. Working Paper No 43. Cambridge, MA: Joint Center for Urban Studies of MIT and Harvard University.

Ribot, Jesse C., Agrawal, Arun, & Larson, Anne M. (2006). Recentralizing while decentralizing: How national governments reappropriate forest resources. *World Development*, 34(11), 1864–1886.

Rondinelli, Dennis A. (1981). Government decentralizatiobn in comparative perspective: Theory and practice in developing countries. *International Review of Administrative Sciences*, 47(2), 133–145.

Rondinelli, Dennis A., & Cheema, G. Shabbir (1983). Implementing decentralization policies. In G. S. Cheema, & D. A. Rondinelli (Eds.), *Decentralization and Development: Policy Implementation in Developing Countries*. Beverly Hills, CA: Sage Publications.

Rondinelli, Dennis A., & Nellis, John (1986). Assessing decentralization policies in developing countries: The case for cautious optmism. *Development Policy Review*, 4(1), 3–23.

Ross, Lester (1992). The politics of environmental protection in the People's Republic of China. *Policy Studies Journal*, 20(4), 628–642.

Runte, Alfred (1997). *National Parks: The American Experience* 3rd ed. Lincoln, NE: University of Nebraska Press.

Sabatier, Paul A. (1986). Top-down and bottom-up approaches to implementation research: A critical analysis and a suggested synthesis. *Journal of Public Policy*, 6(1), 21–48.

Salih, M. A. Mohamed (1999). Introduction: Environmental planning, policies and politics in Eastern and Southern Africa. In A. Mohamed Salih and Shibru Tedla (Eds.), *Environmental Planning, Policies and Politics in Eastern and Southern Africa*. London: Macmillan.

Sayer, J. A. (1981). Tourism or conservation in the National Parks of Benin. *Parks*, 5(4), 13–15.

Sectur, Secretaria de Cultura e Turismo (1999). Table with list of projects carried out under Sectur.

SEI, Superintendência de Estudos Economicos e Sociais da Bahia (1995). *Celulose e Turismo no Extremo Sul da Bahia*. Salvador, Brazil: SEI.

Sekhar, N. U. (1998). Crop and livestock depredation caused by wild animals in protected areas: The case of Sariska Tiger Reserve, Rajasthan, India. *Environmental Conservation*, 25(2), 160–171.

Shams, Rasul (1995). Environmental policy and interest groups in developing countries. *Intereconomics*, 30(1), 16–24.

Siry, Jacek P., Cubbage, Frederick W., & Ahmed, Miyan Rukunuddin (2005). Sustainable forest management: Global trends and opportunities. *Forest Policy and Economics*, 7(4), 551–561.

Souza, Celina (1996). Redemocratization and decentralization in Brazil: The strength of member states. *Development and Change*, 27, 529–555.

Stake, Robert E. (1995). *The Art of Case Study Research*. Thousand Oaks, CA: Sage Publications.

Stem, C. J., Lassoie, J. P., Lee, D. R., & Deshler, D. J. (2003). How 'eco' is ecotourism? A comparative case study of ecotourism in Costa Rica. *Journal of Sustainable Tourism*, 11(4), 322–347.

Stevis, Dimitris (1992). The politics of Greek environmental policy. *Policy Studies Journal*, 20(4), 695–711.

Stræde, Steffen, & Treue, Thorsten (2006). Beyond buffer zone protection: A comparative study of park and buffer zone products' importance to villagers living inside Royal Chitwan National Park and to villagers living in its buffer zone. *Journal of Environmental Management*, 78(3), 251–267.

SUDENE, Superintendência de Desenvolvimento do Nordeste (1999). Retrieved September 21, 1999, from SUDENE's Web page: http://www.sudene.gov.br.

Tendler, Judith (1997). *Good Governments in the Tropics*. Baltimore, MD: Johns Hopkins University Press.

Tisdell, C. A. (1995). Issues in biodiversity conservation including the role of local communities. *Environmental Conservation*, 22(3), 216–22.

Tosato, José A., Maia, Milene, & Braga, Marlon (1997). *Subsídios para Implantação da Secretaria de Meio Ambiente Porto Seguro/Bahia*. Manuscript. Report supporting the creation of a municipal environmental agency. January 3.

Tyler, Charles (1989). A phenomenal explosion. *Geographical Magazine*, August, 18–21.

Uhlig, Christian (1992). Environmental protection and economic policy decisions in developing countries. *Intereconomics*, March/April.

UNEP, United Nations Environment Programme (2004). Database of the United Nations List of Protected Area. Retrieved November 8, 2004, from UNEP Web page: http://sea.unep-wcmc.org/wdbpa/unlist/.

UNEP, United Nations Environment Programme & WTO—World Tourism Organization (1992). *Guidelines: Development of National Parks and Protected Areas for Tourism*. Madrid: UNEP & WTO.

USAID, United States Agency for International Development (1979). *Environmental and Natural Resource Management in Developing Countries. Volume I: Report*. Washington, D.C.: Department of State.

U.S. Department of the Interior, National Park Service (1975). *Preserving Our Natural Heritage. Volume I: Federal Activities*. Washington, D.C.: Government Printing Office.

Van Meter, Donald, & Van Horn, Carl E. (1975). The policy implementation process. *Administration and Society*, 6(4), 445–488.

126   Bibliography

Villamor, Grace B. (2006). The rise of protected area policy in the Philippine forest policy: An analysis from the perspective of Advocacy Coalition Framework (ACF). *Forest Policy and Economics*, 9(2), 162–178.

Viola, Eduardo (1992). O Movimento Ambientalista no Brasil (1971–1991): Da denúncia e conscientização pública para a institucionalização e o desenvolvimento sustentável. *Ciências Sociais Hoje.*

Vyas, V. S., & Reddy, V. Ratna (1998). Assessment of environmental policies and policy implementation in India. *Economic and Political Weekly*, January 10, 48–54.

Wallace. G. N. (1993). Visitor management: Lessons from Galapagos National Park. In K. Lindberg and D. E. Hawkins (Eds.), *Ecotourism: A Guide for Planners and Managers*, (pp. 55–82). North Bennington VT: Ecotourism Society.

Weaver, David B. (1999). Magnitude of ecotourism in Costa Rica and Kenya. *Annals of Tourism Research*, 26(4), October, 792–816.

Wells, Michael (1996). The social role of protected areas in the New South Africa. *Environmental Conservation*, 23(4), 322–331.

Wells, Michael (1997). *Economic Perspectives on Nature Tourism, Conservation and Development. Environment Department Paper No. 55.* Washington D.C.: World Bank.

Wilkinson, Pete (1992). Tourism—curse of the nineties? Belize—an experiment to integrate tourism and the environment. *Community Development Journal*, 27(4), 386–395.

World Bank (1992). *World Bank Development Report 1992: Development and the Environment.* New York: Oxford University Press.

WTO—World Tourism Organization (1999) *International Financial Statistics— Yearbook.* Madrid: WTO.

WTO & UNEP, World Tourism Organization & United Nations Environment Program (1992). *Guidelines: Development of National Parks and Protected Areas for Tourism.* Madrid: WTO and UNEP.

WWF (1994). *Workshop: Diretrizes Políticas para Unidades de Conservação.* Brasilia: WWF.

Xu, Jianying, Chen, Liding, Lu, Yihe, & Fu, Bojie (2006). Local people's perceptions as decision support for protected area management in Wolong Biosphere Reserve, China. *Journal of Environmental Management*, 78(4), 362–372.

Yin, Robert K. (1994). *Case Study Research: Design and Methods.* vol. 5, 2nd ed. Applied Social Research Methods Series. Thousand Oaks, CA: Sage Publications.

Ylhäisi, Jussi (2003). Forest privatisation and the role of community in forests and nature protection in Tanzania. *Environmental Science & Policy*, 6(3), 279–290.

Index

Loureiro, Maria Rita, 34, 50
Loxahatchee National Wildlife Refuge, 50
Lu, Yihe, 32
Lurie, Susan, 21
Lutzenberger, Jose, 14, 16, 110

MacKinnon, J., 26, 27, 29, 35, 36, 37,
  38, 40, 41, 42, 43, 44, 98
Madagascar, 39
Mahanty, Sanghamitra, 19, 20, 21, 42, 43
Mahar, Dennis J., 110
Maia, Milene, 81
mainstream development policy, 8
managed resource protected area, 28
management council, 67
Manor, James, 14, 15, 16, 92, 98, 110
Maputo Elephant Reserve, 45
Mater Natura (Instituto de Estudos
  Ambientais), 63, 64
Mathieson, A., 46
May, Peter H., 66
May, V., 46
Mazmanian, Daniel A., 17, 18
McNeely, Jeffrey A., 7, 31, 34, 35, 36,
  42, 43
Mexico, 26, 46
Middle Age, 26
Migdal, Joel S., 18
Ministério do Meio Ambiente, 54, 114
Ministry of Economy, Treasury and
  Planning, 59
Ministry of the Environment, 51, 52 114
monitoring, 16, 31, 40, 74, 101
Monte Pascoal National Park, 30, 42
Moran, Emilio F., 16, 110
Morell, David, 16
Morse, Bradford, 110
Morse, Stephen, 20
Mozambique, 45
Munasinghe, Mohan, 29
Municipality (ies), 4, 16, 22, 37, 44, 49,
  51, 52, 65, 66, 68, 74, 77, 80, 81, 98,
  99, 100–102, 110, 114

Najam, Adil, 17, 18, 91
Nanne, Kaike, 62
Nash, Roderick, 26, 27, 32, 33, 35, 38,
  42, 49

national park(s), 5, 25, 27, 28, 29, 30,
  31, 32, 33, 34, 35, 37, 38, 41, 42, 47,
  49, 50, 52, 53, 65, 68, 110
natural monument, 28, 29, 54, 111
nature reserve, 28, 29
nature-based tourism, 3, 6, 8, 47, 48, 67,
  82, 94, 104, 105, 106, 113
Nellis, John, 16, 99
Nepal, 50
Nepal, Sanjay K., 50
New Hampshire, 37
New York, 26, 27, 111
Nogueira Neto, Paulo, 34, 54
Nongovernmental organizations
  (NGOs), 5, 31, 44, 51, 62, 63, 64, 67,
  73, 76, 83, 100, 105, 110, 112
nongovernamental group, 22, 100, 102,
  114
Northeastern Brazil, 3
NPS (National Park Service), 35, 38, 49

Obidzinski, Krystof, 33
obstacles, 1, 2, 3, 5, 6, 7, 9, 18, 20, 21,
  23, 25, 27, 29, 31, 32, 33, 35, 37, 39,
  41, 43, 45, 47, 49, 51, 53, 54, 55, 57,
  59, 61, 63, 65, 67, 69, 71, 73, 75, 77,
  79, 81, 83, 85, 87, 88, 89, 90, 97, 103,
  104, 105, 106
obstacles to environmental policy
  implementation, 57, 104, 105
obstacles to policy implementation, 3,
  20, 25, 87, 106
ODA (Oversee Development Agency),
  72, 78, 95
Ogata, Maria G., 22, 35, 36, 51, 52, 84,
  113
Oliveira, Joao L. F., 20
organizational arrangement, 5, 40, 55,
  106

Pacheco, Regina S., 50
Padua, J. A., 27, 34, 52
Palumbo, Dennis J., 18
Panayotou, Theodore, 20
Parc National des Volcans, 37
Parry, Taryn R., 15
participation, 7, 14, 21, 30, 40, 43, 45,
  58, 68, 81, 112